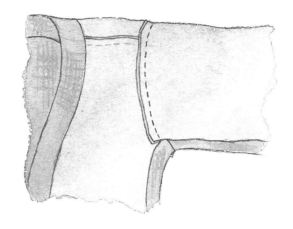

the essentials of sewing

volume 2

the essentials of sewing

volume 2

Miriam Coe

Photography by Debbie Patterson

Clarkson Potter/Publishers
New York

page 1: Jacket (see page 88)
page 2: Bags (see page 38)
page 3: Shirt (see page 65)
page 5: Duvet Cover (see page 30)

llustrations • Lucy Su
Technical drawings • Stephen Dew
Detail photography • Dave King

Text, design and layout copyright © 1996 Quadrille Publishing Limited
Project photography copyright © 1996 Debbie Patterson
Detail photography copyright © 1996 Dave King

Published by Clarkson N. Potter/Publishers, 201 East 50th Street, New York, NY 10022. Member of the Crown Publishing Group.

Random House, Inc. New York, Toronto, London, Sydney, Auckland
http://www.randomhouse.com

CLARKSON N. POTTER, POTTER, and colophon are trademarks of Clarkson N. Potter, Inc.

Originally published in Great Britain by Quadrille Publishing Limited in 1996.

Manufactured in Spain.

Library of Congress Cataloging-in-Publication data is available upon request.

ISBN 0-517-88767-3

10 9 8 7 6 5 4 3 2 1

First American Edition

contents

Introduction

Not long ago, home sewing was an essential skill for all women, and most homes included a sewing machine. While embroidery was a hobby, sewing was simply a job that had to be done.

Times have certainly changed. We now live our lives at an incredible pace, and the time that once was available for sewing has vanished. With the widespread availability of a huge variety of relatively inexpensive, mass-produced garments and home furnishings, the need has also disappeared – but there is another change in the air. Many people are coming back to sewing, but this time from choice and with the desire to make an individual statement in the way they dress and furnish their homes. Most importantly, they are finding renewed enjoyment in sewing, since instead of having to make everything, they can now select particular projects to stitch.

This book is designed to inspire those who already have a basic understanding of sewing and are looking for the skills to progress a little further. The first chapter looks at the characteristics of particular fabrics and the sewing equipment you will need. Some knowledge of equipment and fabrics is essential to successful sewing; it is heartbreaking to put in hours of work only to find that the finished item is a disaster simply because it has been made in an inappropriate fabric.

Next comes seaming. This is the very foundation of sewing, and the end result depends on good work at this stage. It is important to choose the right seam for each job, so a good range of flat seams is covered, plus three-dimensional construction and the use of gussets.

The following chapter looks at the important topic of fabric fullness and how to control and distribute it through the use of gathers, pleats, and tucks.

The final chapter deals with edges and finishings, and ways in which you can embellish your work. This is the point at which you can let your imagination run free, using traditional trimmings in new and interesting ways to make a finished item that is truly your own.

Getting started

Successful sewing depends on choosing the right fabric, so before you pick up a needle it is essential to learn all about the different types and how to choose the right fabric for your project. Go and look at fabrics in the shops and handle them to become familiar with how they behave. Crush a corner of a fabric in your hand and let it unfold gently to see how it reacts; run it through your fingers and see how it feels. Before long you will be able to choose the right fabric for the job simply from its appearance and handling.

In this chapter we look at the origins of each fabric and how it is made, then describe its advantages and disadvantages and how to decide on the right one for a particular design. We also explain how to select exactly the right equipment to turn this fabric into a wonderful piece of stitching of which you can feel justly proud.

fabrics

The finished appearance, feel, and behavior of any fabric depends on the fiber or mix of fibers from which it is made, the way in which the fabric is constructed, and any finishing processes that have been used. Fibers can be divided into two main groups – natural and man-made. The natural fibers can be subdivided into those derived from animal and those from vegetable sources. The man-made fibers can be subdivided into those derived from natural and those derived from chemical sources.

Choosing fabrics

The range of fabrics available today is enormous, and the task of making the right choice can be daunting. Before going out to buy fabric, decide what weight and type would be suitable for the job. Each roll of fabric should be labeled with its fiber content and care instructions, but if in doubt, always ask for details before making your purchase.

Wool

Wool is a natural fabric made from yarn spun from the fleece or hair of a variety of animals including sheep, goats, alpaca, and camels. It is available in a wide range of weights, textures, weaves, and qualities. Wool fabric can be smooth, plain, fleecy, textured, tweedy, crisp, thick, heavy, soft, or fine and delicate, depending on the effect desired. The description "wool" used alone usually means that the fabric has been made from the fleece of a sheep – the other animal fibers are labeled with their names.

Worsted yarns, spun from the longer fibers, are smooth, tightly twisted, and slightly stretchy and are woven into high-quality, durable worsted fabric. Woolen yarns, spun from the shorter fibers, are softer, looser, and slightly twisted, and are made into fabrics such as flannel.

Wool is an easy-to-work and flexible fabric. It can be molded into shape more easily than any other fabric. With careful use of pressing, wool garments can be made to follow the body's curved contours, and tailors make use of these properties when creating well-fitting suits and coats.

Woolen fabrics vary greatly, from the blanket-thick wool velours to delicate wool challis and nun's veiling. Not only is wool warm and comfortable to wear, it is also extremely beautiful. No other fabric can compare with the wonderful wool tweeds so popular with today's top designers.

ADVANTAGES
● Wool is the warmest of all natural fabrics. The intrinsic crimp in the fibers traps air, which – being a bad conductor of heat – helps prevent body heat from escaping.
● Wool fibers are naturally flame resistant; the fibers smolder rather than burst into flame.
● The fibers' natural crimp allows them to resist wrinkling and return to their original shape after creasing.
● Wool fabric tailors well and is easy to shape using steam. Lightweight woolen fabrics are soft and will hang and drape well.
● The fibers hold color well and can be dyed at any stage: fiber, yarn, or fabric.

DISADVANTAGES
● Wool fibers are weaker when wet, and unless specially treated, may shrink. Care must be taken when washing. It may need to be dry-cleaned.
● Moths and carpet beetles attack wool, so precautions need to be taken when storing woolen fabrics.
● Light-colored wool will become discolored by strong light, eventually deteriorating from prolonged exposure.
● Wool fabric can be expensive, so it is often blended with other fibers to reduce the cost and to add strength and shrink resistance. Blending can also help reduce the slightly itchy feel of coarse wool fabric, which may irritate sensitive skins.

Other animal fibers

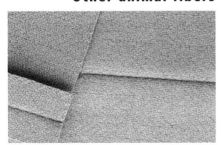

Mohair Mohair comes from the coat of the Angora goat. The lightweight fibers are long and resilient and have an attractive sheen. Mohair fabric tends to be hairy in texture but it dyes very well – bright jewel colors are often used. The fibers are also blended with wool to produce men's lightweight suiting fabrics.

Angora This soft, fluffy fiber comes from the fur of the Angora rabbit and is distinguished from mohair by its sprinkling of white hairs.

Cashmere Obtained from the Cashmere goat, this fiber produces a soft, luxurious fabric with a smooth, slippery feel. Pure cashmere is very expensive, and so it is often blended. Cashmere is very warm, yet light to wear.

Camel's hair Camel-hair fabric is made from the soft inner coat of the camel. It is warm, light, soft to the touch, and very expensive, but the fibers may be blended with wool to reduce the cost. Camel's hair is nearly always camel colored, ranging from creams to golden tans, through to brown. The term "camel cloth" is often used loosely to describe camel-colored coating that is made of wool and not camel and does not have the properties of real camel's hair.

Llama, alpaca, and vicuna These closely related animals produce very soft, fine hair. Fibers from all of them are very expensive and much sought after, as they make beautiful, luxurious fabrics. Again, they can be blended with wool or other fibers for economy.

11

Cotton

Fabric has been produced from the soft, downy seedpod fibers of the cotton plant for thousands of years and, even with the introduction of synthetics, is still the main textile used throughout the world. It is relatively cheap to produce and is a wonderfully easy-going fabric.

The quality of the fabric depends on fiber length, which in turn depends on both the plant variety and growing conditions. The longest fibers are the most expensive and produce the softest fabric. Sea Island, Egyptian, and Pima cotton are some of the finest, while Indian cotton, with shorter fibers, produces a coarser cloth.

Cotton fabric varies from the lightest batiste to the heaviest drill. It is also successful as a knitted fabric, such as cotton jersey, which is used extensively for T-shirts and jogging suits. Cotton is very easy to sew, so if you have never made anything before, this is the fabric with which to start.

ADVANTAGES

• Strong and hardwearing, cotton is easy to wash, can be boiled and srubbed to remove heavy soiling, and does not lose strength when wet.

• Cotton fabric takes up and holds dyes well. It can also be woven or printed with colorful patterns.

• Soft, non-abrasive, and absorbent, cotton is an ideal fabric for wearing next to the skin.

• Cotton fabric does not build up static cling, unlike synthetic fibers.

DISADVANTAGES

• Cotton creases in use, the creases remaining until they are ironed or washed out. This can largely be overcome by blending with synthetics.

• Cotton fabric is flammable and will flare when set aflame, so choose one that has been specially treated to be flame resistant when making nightwear and children's garments.

Linen

Linen is one of the oldest fabrics, yet is still highly prized today for suits and shirts. It is made from the stem fibers of the flax plant, which grows well in cool, damp climates – the best linen comes from Ireland or Belgium.

There is not a great variety of fabrics produced from linen, and most of the variations depend on the degree of coarseness and fineness. Very fine linen is referred to as handkerchief linen, while heavier linens are used for suits and jackets. Linen is also used for lace and embroidery. The fabric is easy to sew and presses beautifully. There is something extra special about neatly pressed, crisp, white linen.

ADVANTAGES

• Linen is cool and absorbent, and is very comfortable to wear, especially in hot weather.

• It is extremely hardwearing and works well for outer garments, curtains, and all types of furniture coverings.

• Linen fabrics have an attractive natural luster and good shape retention, and are moth resistant.

DISADVANTAGES

• Linen creases easily, but can be treated with a crease-resistant finish to help avoid this problem.

• Pure linen is expensive, but can be mixed with cotton and synthetic fibers to reduce the cost and add a measure of crease resistance. Linen combined with cotton is a popular choice for home furnishings.

Other plant fibers

Ramie, also called "China grass", is a soft, hairy fiber that looks like linen but is less expensive and easier to dye. It is usually blended with cotton or silk to make a lustrous fabric.

Jute, hemp, sisal, coir, and kapok are also plant fibers. The first four are used to make floor coverings and rope, while kapok is used as a filling in upholstery.

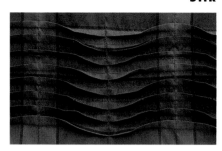

Silk

Silk must be the queen of fabrics, and is probably the most luxurious and highly prized of all natural fibers. The silk is obtained from the caterpillar of the silk moth, which extrudes the threads from its head to wind around itself forming a cocoon. This fabric is unthreaded by man to make into silk fabric. Silk is one of the oldest fibers known to man and has been in continuous production for several thousand years.

Using different weaves, finishes and chemical treatments, silk can be made into a huge variety of different fabrics. It is difficult to believe that heavily textured silk tweed comes from the same source as the floaty, delicate chiffons, or that luxuriously smooth duchesse satin belongs to the same family as crisp, rustling taffeta.

Some silks can be expensive. The quality of the silk itself, together with the quality of the printing and exclusivity of the design, all contribute to the cost. However, there are silks to suit everyone's budget and good-quality silk is available at very reasonable prices.

The best silk is made from the long unbroken silk threads. If the threads break the short lengths are spun together to make spun silk.

Any waste silk from the cocoon is collected and spun into coarser yarns which are woven into heavier fabrics such as silk tweed. These fabrics do not have the drapability or sheen of more expensive silk. Wild silk, also known as tussore, tussah, or shantung, is made from the silk produced by wild silkworms and has characteristic slubs running through the finished fabric.

Some silks may seem difficult to sew at first, but with a little bit of experience these difficulties are soon overcome and the end result makes all the effort more than worthwhile.

ADVANTAGES
- Silk fabrics are smooth, lustrous, and attractive for both dressmaking and home furnishings.
- Although it can look delicate, silk is surprisingly strong.
- Silk is absorbent, which makes it comfortable to wear, and is also resistant to creasing.
- Silk dyes easily, producing vivid colors.
- Silk is light in weight, making it suitable for traveling.

DISADVANTAGES
- Some silk fabrics fray badly when they are cut, and sheer silks such as chiffon and georgette can also be quite difficult to sew.
- Silk requires great care when it comes to laundering.

Man-made fabrics

"Man-made" fabrics include those made from natural sources, such as wood pulp and waste cotton, which are unspinnable in their raw state. They are treated chemically and made into a liquid, which is then forced through holes and dried into a yarn, ready to make into fabric.

Viscose Viscose was one of the first man-made fibers to be produced in this country. Produced from cellulose, viscose was formerly known as rayon. It has been improved greatly in recent years and now has good draping qualities. It is widely used for dresses and skirts, and is also mixed with other fibers, such as wool and cotton.

Acetate Acetate was the second man-made fabric to appear on the market. It is made from waste cotton and/or cellulose. It is not very strong. It is made into taffetas, satins, and brocades. Linings are often made from acetate. Synthetic fibers are made from substances that do not naturally form fibers but are synthesized. The main raw materials for these fibers are oil and petroleum products, and they are produced in much the same way as other man-made fibers.

Synthetic fabrics have progressed a long way since they were first introduced. Their great advantage is their ease of care. They are crease-resistant, and can be crumpled up into a tiny space and emerge without a crease; this makes them ideal traveling. Most synthetic fabrics are also easy to wash, quick to dry, and do not need ironing, a real bonus with today's hectic lifestyles.

Nylon Nylon was the first truly synthetic fiber to be produced. It is very strong and fine. Nylon is used extensively in clothing fabrics, soft furnishings, and upholstery.

Polyester One of the most versatile of the synthetic fibers, polyester is extremely strong and can be made into the finest of fabrics as well as some of the heaviest. It is often mixed with other fibers. Poly-cotton is perhaps the most well known mixture.

Acrylic Acrylic fibers are made from acrylonitrile. The fibers are soft and can be crimped to resemble wool. They are often used for blankets and knitwear, but acrylic fibers also have many uses for dresses, suits, sportswear, and fleecy linings.

ADVANTAGES
- Synthetic fabrics can be pleated permanently because of their plastic nature, and the pleats will not disappear when washed.
- Most synthetic fabrics are crease-resistant.
- They are also very strong and hardwearing.

DISADVANTAGES
- Synthetics are not quite as comfortable to wear as natural fibers.

equipment

Good equipment is absolutely essential for your work to have a professional-looking finish. It also makes stitching much more pleasurable. There are a few items that are essential in the workbasket, and a lot of gadgets that are helpful for home sewing and dressmaking. Buy the basics first, choosing the best you can afford. If treated with care, your sewing equipment will last for many years.

Pins

Pins can be made from steel, nickel plate, brass, or stainless steel. Always choose the correct pins for the fabric you are using. Store pins in airtight boxes or in pincushions; a magnetic pin tray is useful for picking up dropped pins. Inspect pins before use and discard any blunt ones that might snag the fabric.

- **General dressmaking pins** For general use on medium- to heavyweight fabrics.
- **Fine pins** Perfect for fine fabrics, but tough fabrics will make them bend.
- **Extra long, extra fine pins** Very long pins for use on most soft bulky fabrics.
- **Ballpoint pins** Round-ended pins for use with knitted fabrics.
- **Glass-headed pins** Expensive, but easy to see and pick up. A longer version is available, which is intended for use with heavier fabrics.
- **Lace pins** Usually made from brass and used when making and stitching lace.

Needles

Several different types of hand-sewing needles are available, each designed for a particular task. Needles come in numbered sizes – the lower the number, the longer and fatter the needle. They must be sharp, so check before stitching and throw away any that are blunt or bent, or which show signs of rust.

You will need to keep a range of "sharps" and "betweens," plus a few "millinery" needles in your workbasket ready for hand sewing. The other needles mentioned below are only required for specialist hand sewing and embroidery.

Sharps Medium-length needles with small, rounded eyes, used for general sewing.

Betweens (quilting needles) Short needles with small eyes, essential for fine hand sewing and tailoring.

Milliner's needles Very long needles, useful for basting and gathering.

Ballpoint needles Designed especially for use with knitted fabrics. The rounded end slides between the threads without snagging, which might cause puckering and unraveling.

Darning needles Long needles, with large eyes that can cope with thick yarns. The length is necessary in order to span holes when darning.

Crewel (embroidery) needles Medium-length embroidery needles, with large, long eyes take several strands of embroidery thread.

Bodkins Short, blunt needles, which can be rounded or flat, with large eyes. Used for threading elastic and ribbon through casings or helping to push out tight corners on collars and cuffs.

Thimbles

To help feed the needle through the fabric, you may like to use a thimble on the middle finger of your sewing hand. Choose a steel thimble in preference to one made from soft, easily pierced silver.

Threads

Choosing the correct thread will insure a professional look and finish to your sewing projects. If possible, the thread should match the composition of the fabric in both fiber and weight, and be able to withstand the same washing and ironing temperatures, since the two elements cannot be treated differently once the project is sewn.

Choose a thread color that matches the fabric. On a two-tone fabric, it is better to match the darker color, because a single thread appears lighter when removed from the spool. Threads for both hand and machine sewing should be strong and of good quality, with a smooth finish. The higher the number on the spool, the finer the thread.

Beeswax is a useful addition to your workbasket. Pull the working thread through it to give the thread extra strength and to prevent tangling when hand sewing.

Linen Very strong, and useful for sewing on buttons, but often linen is too thick and too expensive for general sewing.

Silk Wonderfully smooth and shiny, but very expensive. Silk thread is ideal for stitching pure silk and is also good for sewing woolen garments, particularly for hand stitching. Thick silk threads are ideal for hand-sewn buttonholes.

Cotton The most common of the natural threads. Less expensive than silk or linen, it is usually "mercerized" to make it smooth. Cotton and cotton-mix threads are suitable for sewing all natural fabrics.

Synthetic Usually made of polyester, this thread is fine and strong, and suitable for most fabrics.

Basting thread Soft, loosely twisted unmercerized cotton, available in black and white, basting threads break easily This is important, as basting threads need to be removed quickly and easily without tearing the fabric. Basting thread is also quite fuzzy, which allows it to grip the fabric and stay in place until it is ready to be removed.

Invisible thread A nylon thread, virtually colorless to blend with any fabric.

Measuring equipment

You will need a dressmaker's tape measure and a yardstick (meter rule).

Choose a plastic or fiberglass tape measure, but both will need renewing frequently, as they have a tendency to stretch and give inaccurate measurements.

A yardstick (meter rule) available in wood or plastic, is a useful and, in some circumstances, a more accurate tool than a tape measure. Keep plastic rulers clean, and wooden ones free of splinters.

Markers

A variety of fabric markers is available, ranging from special pens whose lines fade in the daylight or after several days, to various types of colored crayon.

One of the best markers is traditional tailor's chalk, which comes in square and triangular shapes. Several colors are available, but white is the easiest to remove, using a brush. For fine, accurate lines, sharpen tailor's chalk using a scissors blade.

Scissors

Scissors must be sharp. They should be kept solely for cutting fabrics and threads, and should not be used for any other crafts since this might blunt them. Try not to drop scissors on the floor, as this will damage the blades. Left-handed scissors are available in all the main types.

Dressmaking shears Essential for cutting out fabric. Invest in a good-quality pair of large, long-bladed shears, and with care, they will last for many years. The handles should be bent to one side, so that while cutting out the shears sit flat on the table. For more advanced work, it is a good idea to have two pairs – one for natural fibers and one for synthetics, as the latter quickly blunt the blades.
General sewing scissors Choose a medium-sized pair with straight handles, for trimming seams.
Small sewing scissors Short, very sharp points on small scissors are essential for snipping threads, and for cutting into buttonholes and sharp corners.
Paper or craft scissors Keeping a pair of ordinary household scissors in your workbasket will remove the temptation to use your fabric scissors for cutting paper or cardboard.
Rotary cutters Very sharp cutting wheels, particularly good for cutting straight pieces of fabric, such as bias strips or patchwork pieces, where accuracy is important. They must only be used with a special cutting mat.

Pressing equipment

Correct pressing is essential to achieve a really professional result, so good pressing equipment is vital. Make sure that the iron and ironing board are kept clean.

• A good heavyweight iron is essential. It can be a steam iron, but you can make steam using a damp press cloth.
• Muslin makes good pres cloths. Cut several, approximately 1m (1yd) square. These can be doubled up to make the required thickness.
• A tailor's ham is useful for pressing anything with a curve, as it will insure that the curve does not flatten out and lose its shape. The ham has wool on one side for pressing woolen fabrics and cotton on the other for cotton fabrics.
• Similar to a ham, a seam roll is used for pressing seams. The iron will exert pressure on the stitches of the seam and not on the seam allowance to avoid making an impression on the right side of the fabric.
• A velvet pressing board will prevent crushing of the pile.
• A simple block of wood can be used to bang steam into a fabric. This technique is used to press in pleats and in tailoring. If a block is not available, use the back of a clothes brush.

sewing machines

Sewing machines have not only revolutionized home sewing but also enabled the mass production of ready-made clothes. They have become very sophisticated machines with a wide range of different models on the market, so choosing the right one can be a daunting task. A sewing machine is a costly investment, but choose wisely and it will last a lifetime.

Sergers can stitch, trim, and finish a raw seam edge in one action, producing a professional and store-bought finish. With a sewing machine and a serger working side-by-side you can create a wealth of beautiful things.

Sewing machines

With the wealth of electronic and computerized models available today, choosing a sewing machine can be difficult, and requires time and careful attention. Collect brochures and talk to other sewers; go to a reputable independent dealer, explain your sewing needs, and ask for advice. Try any machine you are considering yourself – a demonstrator can make every machine look easy to operate. Try threading the machine yourself, and change the bobbin and the needle. Take some of your own fabric with you, as a demonstrator will use easy fabrics.

Do not be taken in by all the special features in the sewing machine: think realistically about your sewing needs and how many of these elaborate functions you will actually need in your stitching projects. Most people simply need a machine that will give them a good straight stitch, zigzag stitch, and buttonhole.

Machine needles

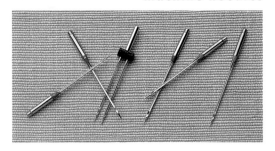

It is important to use the correct needle for each sewing project. It is also important to change needles frequently – machine needles become blunt surprisingly quickly, and as a result affect the smooth running of the machine. Various problems can then arise, including skipped stitches and snagged fabric. The timing of the machine can also be affected, so get into the habit of changing the needle before starting each new project.

Machine needles are available in numbered sizes. The lower the number, the finer the needle.

US/English	8	10	12	14	16
Continental	60	70	80	90	100

A 8 (60) needle is recommended for the finest fabrics, such as silk chiffon, a 16 (100) needle is suitable for the heaviest work.

A range of specialist needles for sewing machines is also available.

Overlockers can use sewing machine needles or may require specialist needles, so check with the manufacturer.

Ballpoint needle Specially designed for knitted rather than woven fabrics, with a rounded end instead of a sharp point. The blunt end feeds between the threads instead of puncturing them, minimizing the risk of unraveling.

Jeans needle Very sharp point for penetrating thick, closely woven fabrics, such as denim, sailcloth, and ticking.

Wedge-point needle Arrow-shaped point to pierce tough leather and vinyl.

Twin needle Two needles on one shank, both of which are threaded. They make two absolutely parallel, equally spaced rows of stitching, perfect for pintucks and topstitching. Twin needles are available with different widths between the needles.

Triple needle Similar to a twin needle, but with three needles on one shank.

Wing needle Has a wide shank and is used for decorative work.

Sergers

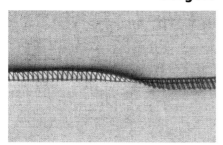

A serger (or overlocking machine) is a relatively recent introduction. It does not take the place of a conventional sewing machine, but is intended to be used alongside it.

The primary function of a serger is to give raw edges a professional finish, neatly trimming off the excess fabric and then immediately overcasting the newly cut raw edges. Seams can thus be sewn, trimmed, and overcast in one operation, saving hours of time. These seams are particularly suitable for knitted fabrics, such as those used for sportswear, because they allow for a certain amount of stretch. They can also be used on woven fabrics with good results. In addition, some sergers can be used for decorative stitching and to make rolled hems on fine fabrics.

Sergers are available with 2, 3, 4, or 5 threads. All sergers cut and overcast edges at the same time, but the 4- and 5-thread machines make an extra row of machine stitching inside the serged edge, creating a more secure seam. This is really necessary on woven fabrics, when it has not been seamed with a conventional sewing machine. Most sergers can be used with fewer threads than their maximum; for example, most 4-thread machines can make 2- or 3-thread overcast edges as well as the 4-thread seam.

Choosing a serger

As when choosing a conventional sewing machine, go to an independent and reputable dealer and explain your sewing needs. Take your own fabrics with you and try several models – sergers are notoriously difficult to thread, so try this out for yourself. You may need to make more than one visit.

Choosing serger threads

Sergers use vast amounts of thread, which is available on huge cones. It is expensive to buy cones of just the right color to match all the different fabrics, so buy colors which blend rather than match, such as creams, beiges, and grays, plus black and white.

Make sure that the thread is strong. It will be put under a lot of strain in the serger, and if it breaks rethreading is very annoying. The thread must also be fine, as the volume of stitching could otherwise make the seams too bulky. Decorative threads are also available.

Plain & fancy seams

Seams are the basis of everything you make, and it is important that you choose the right seam and make that seam as skillfully as possible, as the finished effect depends on it. Saris, sarongs, and throws may not need seams; however these are the exceptions.

Seams are used to join narrow widths of fabrics, for curtains or bed linen. The duvet cover has been made in this way and has straight seams that are disguised and emphasised with broderie anglaise.

Seams can also give shape or form to a garment. The Japanese kimono, shows seams being used to join simple angular shapes to create a comfortable loose-fitting garment. While the skirt seams have been shaped to fit the contour of the body.

Seams are also used to make three-dimensional shapes, and these can incorporate a gusset. The bags and bench cushion use this technique.

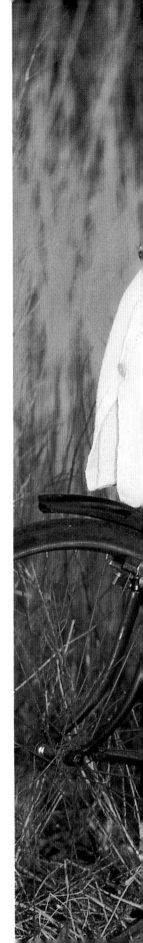

plain seams

Fabrics are seamed or joined together to make a wider piece of fabric or to shape a garment or project. Most seams are therefore functional. When choosing which seam to use, the type of fabric, the article or garment being made, the amount of wear and washing, together with the general finished effect should all be taken into consideration. Different seams can be used in the same project, depending on their position.

Plain, flat seam

This is the most commonly used seam. It is easy to make and gives a good flat finish, but with only one row of stitching it is not very strong. After stitching, the seam allowances are pressed open to either side of the seam.

1 With right sides together and raw edges matching, pin the two pieces of fabric together, placing the pins at right angles to the edge. Baste the two fabrics together along the seam line.

2 Machine stitch the fabrics together along the basted seam line. Next remove the basting threads. Press the machine stitching flat, and then press the seam open.

Finishing raw edges

As the raw edges of a plain, flat seam are exposed on the wrong side, they might require finishing to prevent them from fraying and to give a neater appearance. There are various ways of doing this, either by machine or by hand. Check that the method of seam finishing is appropriate to the fabric and project.

Zigzag This simple method of seam finishing is worked on the sewing machine, with a zigzag stitch made over the raw edge. The zigzag width and length can be altered for different effects. This method is especially useful for thick, firm, or knitted fabrics.

Serging This method of seam finishing is worked on an overlocking machine or serger (see page 21), either before or after stitching the seam on an ordinary sewing machine. It is very effective in preventing fraying, especially on silk, and can give quite a professional finish. As the overlocking threads are very fine, the result is a neat finish.

Edge stitching On firm, lightweight fabrics, such as cottons, the raw edges can be machine finished. Turn under ⅛" (3mm) along the raw edge of each seam allowance and press, then stitch close to the folded edge. As there are two layers of fabric, this method is not suitable for thick fabrics.

Hand stitching This is often preferable to machine stitching as a method of finishing. Careful hand stitching will blend in with the fabric and will not distort the seam. Two stitches are generally used:
Overcasting – work from left to right (or right to left), making slanting stitches over the raw edge (fig 1). Do not pull the stitching too tight.
Blanket stitch – work from left to right, insert the needle through the fabric and bring it out under the edge over the working thread. Pull the thread through, forming a stitch on the edge of the seam allowance (fig 2). Again, do not pull the stitching too tight.

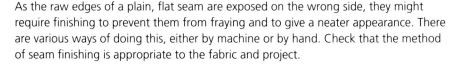

fig 1

fig 2

French seam

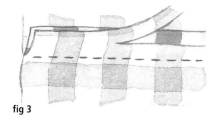

A French seam is self-finishing, as the raw edges are enclosed within. Two rows of machine stitching make this seam stronger than a plain, flat seam.

French seams are only suitable for medium- and lightweight or sheer fabrics, since the extra thickness would be too great on heavier ones. French seams work best on straight seams and are particularly useful on fine fabrics, where the seam allowances would otherwise show through to the right side, for example on chiffon.

1 With wrong sides together and raw edges matching, pin and baste the two pieces of fabric together.
2 Machine stitch the seam with a ⅜" (1cm) seam allowance. Remove the basting threads.
3 Press the stitching flat. Press the seam allowances to one side, and then trim them down to ⅛" (3mm).

4 Refold the seam with the right sides of the fabric together, and using finger and thumb, manipulate the fabric so that the machine stitching is right on the folded edge. Pin, baste, and stitch ¼" (6mm) from the folded edge.
5 Remove the basting stitches. Press the machine stitching, and then press the seam to one side.

Flat-fell seam

This is a very useful self-finishing seam. It uses two rows of machine stitching, so is very strong. A flat-fell seam lies flat and looks as neat on the wrong side of the fabric as on the right side.

1 With right sides together and raw edges matching, pin, baste, and stitch the two pieces of fabric together as for a plain, flat seam. Remove the basting, and press the seam flat.
2 Trim one of the seam allowances to ¼" (6mm) (fig 3). Press both seam allowances to one side, with the trimmed one underneath. Insure that

you are consistent throughout, pressing the seams to either the front or the back.
3 Fold the raw edge of the wider seam allowance over and under the narrow one (fig 4), and baste this folded edge to the main fabric.
4 Stitch close to the folded edge, keeping parallel with the first row of stitches (fig 5). Remove the basting.

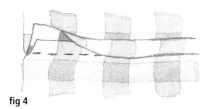

fig 3

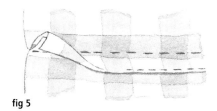

fig 4

fig 5

Traditional flat-fell seam

The traditional flat-fell seam is worked on the right side of the fabric so that both rows of machine stitching are visible. The stitching can be worked in a contrasting color for added decoration.

It is very important that the two rows of stitching look exactly the same, so use the same stitch size throughout. As the upper and lower stitches on the machine are not exactly the same, care must be taken to insure that it is the lower thread that is folded out of sight and the upper thread that is visible on the right side.

To make the seam, follow the instructions for the flat-fell seam above, but begin by placing the wrong sides of the fabric together.

decorative seams

Seams are functional, but they can also be decorative and with a bit of imagination can be made a feature of the project. Making a seam more conspicuous often involves using another row of stitching, and this immediately makes the seam stronger. Note that when working a line of machine stitching on the right side of a garment or home decorating project, care must be taken to be very accurate, insuring that the distance from the seam line to the stitching is consistent throughout.

Welt seam

This is a variation on the flat-fell seam and is used on heavier fabrics where a flat-fell seam would be too bulky. The extra row of stitching is visible from the right side and adds both strength and decoration.

1 With right sides together and raw edges matching, pin, baste, and stitch the two pieces of fabric together as for a plain, flat seam. Remove the basting, and press the seam to one side.
2 Trim the inner seam allowance to ¼" (6mm). Zigzag the raw edge of the wider seam allowance if necessary (fig 1).
3 Working on the right side, baste through the fabric and the wider seam allowance, enclosing the trimmed edge. Again working on the right side, topstitch beside the seam (fig 2), catching in the wider seam allowance.

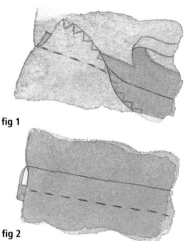

fig 1

fig 2

Tucked and lapped seams

Tucked and lapped seams are made in the same way. They are both strong and decorative, with the final row of stitching on the right side. On a lapped seam, the stitching is close to the fold; on a tucked seam, ¼" (6mm) from the fold.

1 Mark seam lines on both fabrics.
2 Turn the seam allowance of the top fabric to the wrong side. Press and baste.
3 Place the top fabric on the bottom fabric, matching the folded edge to the marked seam line. Pin and baste in position. Stitch, parallel to and ⅛"–¼" (3–6mm) from the fold (fig 3).

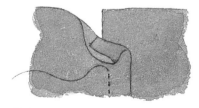

fig 3

Topstitched seam

This is a variation on a plain, flat seam, with two rows of stitching added on either side of the seam line for decoration.

1 With right sides together and raw edges matching, pin, baste, and stitch the two pieces of fabric together as for a plain, flat seam. Press the seam open.
2 With the right side of the seam facing upward, topstitch the required distance from the seam along one side.
3 Working in the same direction, repeat on the other side of the seam, making sure the distance from the seam to the topstitching is the same. Use the presser foot as a guide to position the stitching.

Piped seam

There are two kinds of piped seam – soft and corded. Piping consists of a strip of fabric folded lengthwise, which is sewn into a seam so that the fold of the piping is visible for decoration. If it is to be inserted into a curved or shaped seam, the fabric strip will need to be cut out on the bias. Filler cord of various thicknesses can be sewn into the piping before it is stitched into a seam for a more defined look.

Soft piped seam

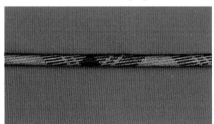

1 Fold the fabric strip in half lengthwise with wrong sides together. Place the folded piping on the right side of one of the pieces of the fabric. Pin and baste along the seam line (fig 4).

fig 4

2 Place the second piece of fabric over the first, with right sides together and raw edges matching. Pin, baste, and machine stitch along the seam line (fig 5). Remove the basting and press.

fig 5

Corded piped seam

A corded piped seam is made in the same way as a soft piped seam, but a length of cord is inserted inside the fold of the fabric strip. This is basted and stitched in place before the corded piping is attached to the main fabric (fig 6). A zipper foot, or special piping foot, on the machine will enable you to stitch close to the cord, giving a better finish.

fig 6

Insertion seam

For this decorative seam, the fabrics to be joined are positioned at a distance from each other and bridged by a specially designed insertion, which is usually made of lace or broderie anglaise (eyelet). If the insertion has a specially finished edge, it is usually positioned on top of the fabric so that the edge can be seen. If it does not have an attractive edge, it is placed behind the fabric. Insertion seams can be straight or zigzag stitched. A mock inseertion is made by covering a seam with broderie anglaise.

Straight-stitch insertion
1 Make a narrow hem on the edge of both pieces of fabric.
2 Lay the insertion on top of the right side of the pieces of fabric. Pin, baste, and stitch in place.

Zigzag-stitch insertion
1 Lay the insertion right side up on the right side of one piece of fabric so that the edge covers the fabric by ¼" (6mm). Pin and baste.
2 Stitch with a small, closely worked zigzag (fig 7) following any pattern on the edge of the insertion. Trim back the fabric to the zigzag stitches.
3 Lay the other edge of the insertion over the other side of the fabric in the same way. Pin, baste, and zigzag in place (fig 8). Trim away the excess fabric.

fig 7

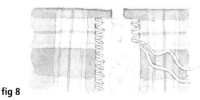

fig 8

bed linen

A fine soft cotton lawn makes the most luxurious bed linen. If fabric widths need to be joined for the duvet cover, you can make a feature of the joins by adding a broderie anglaise insertion to cover the seams.

Square pillowcase with lace insertion

Square pillows are becoming increasingly popular, but there is still only a small choice of ready-made pillowcases in this shape available. The central square of this case is held to the mitered edge with insertion lace, and the whole pillowcase is edged with a deep mitered border.

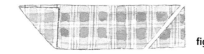

fig 1

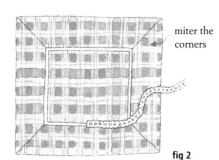

miter the corners

fig 2

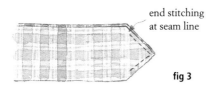

end stitching at seam line

fig 3

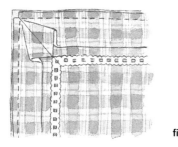

fig 4

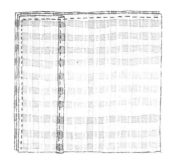

fig 5

You will need
1½yd (1.4m) cotton, 36″ (90cm) wide
1¾yd (1.6m) broderie anglaise eyelet lace, ¾″ (2cm) wide, for insertion
Matching sewing thread
1¾yd (1.6m) gingham ribbon, ¼″ (6mm) wide

To cut out
1 For the front, cut out from cotton fabric 1 piece 14½″ (37cm) square, and 4 pieces each 19¾″ x 3⅛″(50 x 8cm) for the mitered inner border.
2 For the back, cut out from cotton fabric 1 piece 20⅛″ x 19¾″ (51 x 50cm), 1 piece 19¾″ x 6¾″ (50 x 17cm) for the flap, and 4 strips each 23¾″ x 4¾″ (60 x 12cm) for the outer border.

To make the front
1 With the first inner border strip right side uppermost, fold up one end diagonally matching the raw edges, and press. Unfold and cut along the pressed line (fig 1). Miter the other end of the strip in the same way, but so that the raw edge points in the opposite direction. Cut all the border pieces in the same way.
2 With right sides together, join the inner border strips together, taking a ⅜″ (1cm) seam allowance. Press the seams open. Turn in ⅜″ (1cm) along the inner edge, press, and topstitch.
3 Press under ⅜″ (1cm) around the outer edge of the front central square piece, and topstitch close to the folded edge.
4 With the right sides up, place the inner border around the central square, with corners matching. Mitering each corner, pin the broderie anglaise eyelet lace

around the square and border (fig 2), just overlapping the edges of both. Join the ends of the lace. Baste and topstitch the lace along both edges.
5 Thread the gingham ribbon around the insertion and knot the ends together at one corner.

To make and join on the outer border
1 Press the first outer border strip in half lengthwise with wrong sides facing. At each end, fold up the raw edges diagonally to match the folded edge and press. Unfold and cut along the pressed line. Repeat with each border strip.
2 With the strips unfolded and right sides together, join them together to form a square, taking a ⅜″ (1cm) seam allowance (fig 3). Turn to the right side and refold in half. Press.
3 With right sides together, pin and baste the raw edges of the outer border to the pillowcase front (fig 4).

To finish the pillowcase
1 Stitch a double ¼″ (6mm) hem along one long edge of the flap and a double ⅜″ (1cm) hem along one short edge of the back section.
2 Pin the back over the front with right sides together, the back hem edge adjoining the seam line at one side and the remaining raw edges matching.
3 Position the flap over the hemmed edge of the back pillowcase, matching the raw edge to the raw edge of the front and the side edges to the raw edges of the front and back. Pin, baste, and stitch all around (fig 5).
4 Turn the pillowcase right side out, tucking the flap inside, and press.

duvet cover

The seams on the duvet cover need to be strong to withstand wear and tear and repeated washing. By adding a row of mock insertion over each seam, the seams are made strong and secure through the two rows of topstitching that are added.

fig 1

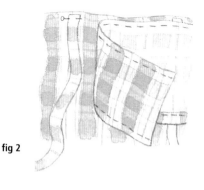

fig 2

fig 3

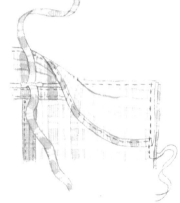

fig 4

You will need

10¾yd (9.7m) main fabric, 36" (90cm) wide

Matching sewing thread

4¾yd (4.5m) broderie anglaise insertion, 2½" (6cm) wide

4¾yd (4.5m) ribbon, ¼" (6mm) wide and safety pin (optional)

To cut out

1 For the front, cut 1 piece 95¼" (237cm) by the fabric width and 2 side front pieces each 95¼" x 10½" (237 x 27cm).

2 For the back, cut 1 piece 81⅛" (206.5cm) by the fabric width and 2 side back pieces each 81⅛" x 10½" (206.5 x 27cm).

3 Cut 10 ties each 10¼" x 1" (26 x 2.5cm).

To make the front

1 Join the side front pieces to the center front piece with a plain, flat seam and finish the seam edge. Cut off a piece of fabric 14" (34cm) deep from the bottom of the front piece for the flap.

2 Place the broderie Anglaise centrally over the seams on the front, right side up. Pin, baste, and stitch in place (fig 1).

3 If adding ribbon, cut it into 2 equal lengths. Fasten one end of the first length to a safety pin, and thread the ribbon through the broderie Anglaise. Repeat for the second length.

4 Make the ties by folding the tie strips in half lengthwise with right sides together and machine stitching ¼" (6mm) from the long raw edges. Turn the ties right side out, and press. Tuck in ¼" (6mm) at one end of each tie and slipstitch to close. Make 5 pairs of ties in the same way.

5 With right sides together and the raw ends of the ties matching the raw edge of the front, pin 5 ties equally spaced along the bottom edge of the front.

6 Make a 1" (2.5cm) hem along one long edge of the flap piece, and stitch in place. Position the flap on the front piece along the bottom edge with right sides together. Pin, baste, and stitch the flap in place, sandwiching the ties in between the front and the flap (fig 2).

To make the back

1 Join the side back pieces to the center back piece in the same way as for the front piece. Press up a 1" (2.5cm) double hem along the bottom edge.

2 Unfold the hem, and with right sides together and the ends of the remaining 5 ties placed to the raw edge of the back, position the ties on the back piece to correspond with the front. Pin and baste the ties, then refold the hem with the ties incorporated (fig 3). Stitch the hem along the fold and along the edge.

To finish the duvet cover

1 With right sides facing, place the front and back pieces of the cover together, keeping the flap out of the way and abutting the hem of the back to the flap seam.

2 Replace the flap over the back, then pin, baste, and stitch the sides and top edge of the cover (fig 4), stitching through the flap sides. Press, and turn the cover right side out. Insert your duvet in the cover; tuck in the flap and fasten the ties.

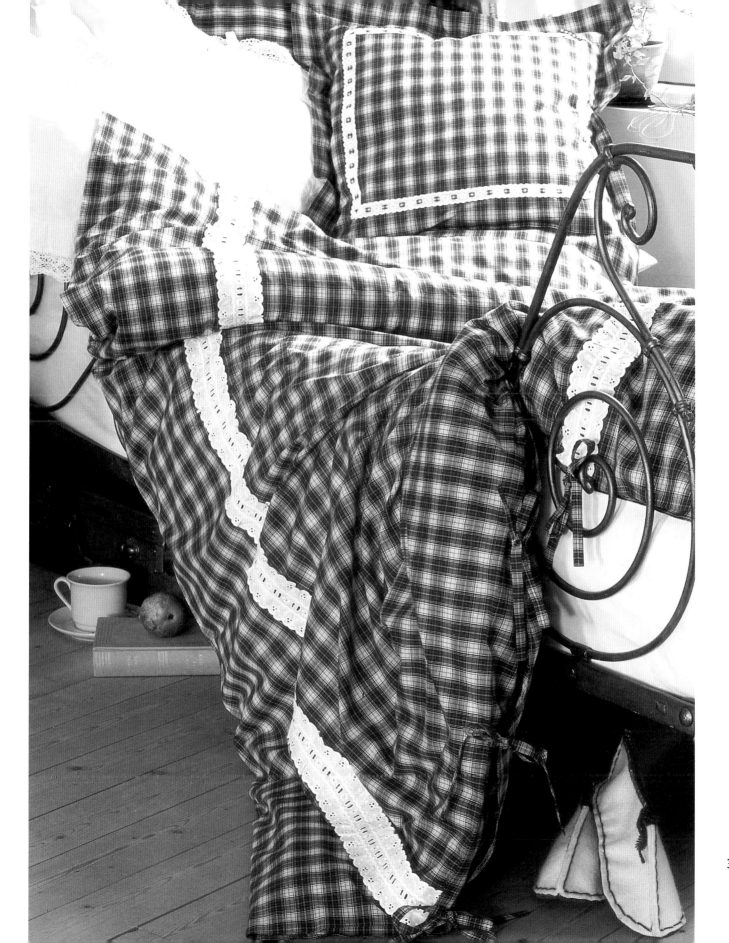

kimono

The kimono originated in Japan. There it is worn for both day and evening. Sometimes kimonos are made in the most sumptuous fabrics. We have adopted the simple shape of the kimono and combined stripes and checks in fashionable red and white, to create the perfect garment for lazy days spent relaxing at home.

You will need

4¼yd (4m) main fabric, 45" (115cm) wide
28" (70cm) contrasting fabric, 36" (90cm) wide
Matching sewing threads
Paper for patterns

To enlarge the patterns

Following the diagrams and using the measurements shown on the shapes below, draw the paper patterns.

To cut out

From main fabric
1 back
2 fronts
2 sleeves
From contrasting fabric
2 cuffs
2 collars
2 sash pieces

To make the hanger and join front and back

1 Cut out a strip of contrasting fabric 4" x 1¼" (10 x 3cm), and fold it in half lengthwise with right sides together. Stitch ¼" (6mm) from the long raw edge. Turn right side out, and press.
2 Fold the strip into an arrow-shaped hanger and position at the center of the neck on the wrong side of back piece, with raw edges matching. Baste the hanger in place (fig 1).

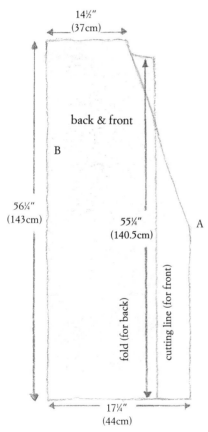

14½"
(37cm)

back & front

B

56¼"
(143cm)

55¼"
(140.5cm)

A

fold (for back)

cutting line (for front)

17¼"
(44cm)

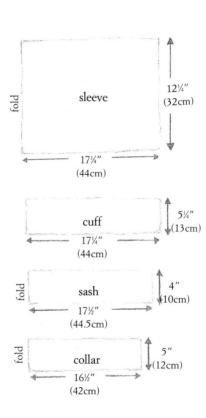

fold

sleeve

12¼"
(32cm)

17¼"
(44cm)

cuff

5¼"
(13cm)

17¼"
(44cm)

fold

sash

4"
(10cm)

17½"
(44.5cm)

fold

collar

5"
(12cm)

16½"
(42cm)

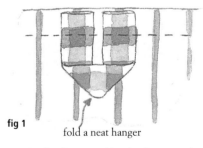

fig 1   fold a neat hanger

3 Join the front and back pieces at the shoulders with French seams.
4 Press a small double ¼" (6mm) hem down the center fronts from point A to the hem edge; stitch in place.

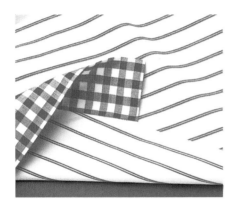

To make and attach the collar

1 Join the 2 collar pieces at the center back, and press. Press the seam allowance on both short edges of the collar to the wrong side.

2 Fold the collar in half lengthwise with wrong sides together and press. Open the fold and press the seam allowance along one of the long edges to the wrong side.

3 With right sides together, join the unpressed long edge of the collar to the main body, matching points A in the front and seam to center back. Press the seam toward the collar and trim the seam allowances if necessary.

4 Refold the collar in half along the pressed fold, taking the collar over to the wrong side of the main body.

5 Abutt the folded seam allowance to the first line of machine stitching. Pin and baste in position, then slipstitch in place, catching the stitches into the machine stitching.

6 Slipstitch the ends of the collar.

To join on the sleeves

1 With right sides together, pin, baste, and stitch one long edge of each cuff to the lower edge of each sleeve. Press the seams toward the cuffs.

2 Join each sleeve to the main body with a French seam, matching the center point at the top of the sleeve with the shoulder seam and stopping ⅝" (1.5cm) from either end of the sleeve (fig 2).

Press the seams toward the sleeves.

3 Join the side seams of the body, stopping at the point B.

4 Join the sleeves, starting at point B and stitching up the ends of the sleeves.

5 Turn under the remaining raw edge of the cuffs and slipstitch in place, catching the stitches into the machine stitching in the same way as for the collar (fig 3).

To make the sash

1 Join the sash pieces. Trim and press.

2 Fold the sash in half lengthwise with right sides together, and stitch the long edges together.

3 Turn the sash right side out, and press with the seam over the center. Turn in the ends and slipstitch in place. Press.

To make the carriers

1 Cut a strip of contrasting fabric 8" x 1½" (20 x 4cm). Fold it in half lengthwise with right sides together, and stitch ¼" (6mm) from the long raw edge. Turn the strip right side out, and press with the seam over the center.

2 Cut the strip into 4" (10cm) lengths. Fold under both ends of each carrier.

3 Pin the carriers in position on the main body, and stitch in place with a square of stitching at each end (fig 4).

To finish the kimono

Turn up a 1" (2.5cm) hem on lower edge; tuck under ¼" (6mm) along the raw edge, and stitch in place.

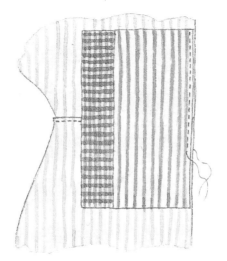

fig 2

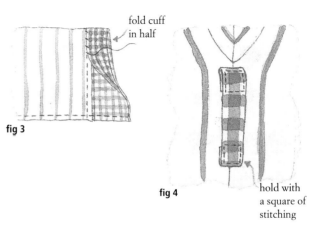

fold cuff in half

fig 3

fig 4

hold with a square of stitching

curves & box shapes

Shaping and depth is achieved with curved seams and gussets. Curved seams need to be stitched with care so that the seam allowance remains constant and the stitching flows smoothly around the shape. Once stitched, the seam allowance must be clipped and notched so that the seam can be pressed flat.

A gusset is the strip of fabric that provides depth between two shaped pieces. It can be as narrow as ¾" (2cm), or wide – say 4" (10cm) on a deep cushion. Gussets can be cut on the straight or on the bias of the fabric, depending on the gusset depth and the effect required. Cut gusset strips in one long length, or in sections to accommodate openings.

Curved seams

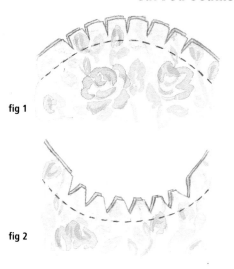

fig 1

fig 2

To make a curved seam, the two fabrics are placed together in the usual way for plain flat seams, using the appropriate seam allowance for the item. Set the sewing machine to a normal straight stitch, and work slowly to achieve the necessary smooth and accurate stitching.

1 Place the two fabrics together with right sides facing, and pin at regular intervals with the pinheads at right angles to the edge. Baste, then stitch with the appropriate seam allowance, feeding the fabric gently through the machine and guiding it around the curved edge.

2 To finish outward curves, cut out evenly spaced notches from the seam allowance so that when the fabric is pressed it can overlap and lie flat (fig 1). To avoid weakening the seam

unnecessarily, stagger the notches on either side of the seam line. Finish the raw edges with a zigzag stitch on the sewing machine.

3 To finish inward curves, where the seam allowance needs to spread out in order to lie flat, clip into the allowance up to the seam line (fig 2). Insure that the clips are regularly spaced, and fit in as many as necessary to allow the seam to be pressed flat. Finish the raw edges of the fabric with a zigzag stitch on the sewing machine.

Circular box shapes

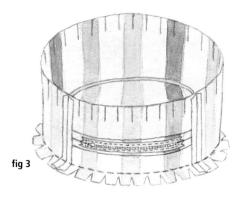

fig 3

Circular box shapes consist of top and bottom sections plus a gusset strip to cover the side edge. On large, circular pieces such as a deep cushion, a zipper can be fitted into a section of the gusset strip before it is inserted between the top and bottom sections.

1 Cut one gusset strip to the circumference of the circle plus twice the seam allowance. With right sides together, join the strip into a ring. Clip the seam allowance along both edges. With right sides facing, pin, baste, and stitch the gusset to the top and bottom pieces, leaving an opening in one seam for turning. Insert the cushion and close the opening.

2 To add a zipper, measure the length of the zipper and cut a gusset strip to size

adding twice the seam allowance, plus four times the seam allowance wider than the required depth.

3 Pin the zipper gusset pieces right sides together, and baste along the whole length. Stitch from each end, leaving a central opening for the zipper. Press the seam open. Pin the zipper over the wrong side of the seam behind the basted section. Baste and stitch around the zipper. Partially open the zipper. Stitch the gusset in place (fig 3).

Box shapes

Box shapes are dealt with in the same way as circular box shapes, with the addition of a gusset strip. On a deep cushion, a zipper is stitched between two folded gusset strips before it is inserted between the top and bottom sections. Deep gussets are usually cut on the straight grain of the fabric and can run all around the shape with just one join, or be fitted together with seams to give sharp, crisp corners.

1 Measure the edges of the shape and cut one gusset strip to the length of each side plus twice the seam allowance by the depth of the shape plus twice the seam allowance.
2 Join the gusset strips together into a square or rectangle, beginning and ending the seams ⅝" (1.5cm) from each edge of each strip.
3 With right sides together, pin, baste, and stitch the top section to the top edge of the gusset strip. Spread open the strip at each corner and then stitch, forming sharp corners.
4 Repeat, to stitch the bottom edge of the gusset strip to the bottom section, leaving a large opening centrally in one

side. Trim, and then turn the cushion cover right side out.
5 Insert the cushion, turn in the opening edges and slipstitch together to close.
6 To set in a zipper, measure the length of the zipper and cut two strips to this length plus twice the seam allowance, by the depth of the shape plus twice the seam allowance. Fold each strip in half lengthwise with wrong sides together and press. Place the zipper in the center of these two pieces, and baste and stitch it in position. Remove the basting. Then make the shape in the same way as before (fig 4), but without leaving an opening. Open the zipper partially before stitching in the gusset strip (fig 5).

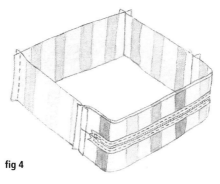

fig 4

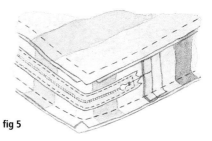

fig 5

Piped boxed shapes

Plain or corded piping is often added on either side of the gusset strip to provide emphasis or a touch of color or pattern to a plain shape. Cut the piping strip on the bias of the fabric.

1 Measure the length of the gusset strip, and make two lengths of piping to this length plus 1½" (4cm) for joining. Pin, baste, and stitch each length of piping around the top and bottom sections.
2 Clip into the piping seam allowance at each corner on square and rectangular shapes. On circular shapes, notch the piping seam allowance all around at

regular intervals so that the piping curves smoothly around the shape.
3 Join the ends of the piping together neatly to fit, positioning the join in the centre of the back on square and rectangular shapes.
4 Join the gusset to the top and bottom sections, and if required, a zipper can be added as before.

37

bags

Bags are an essential part of any wardrobe, whether for traveling or just shopping. A roomy saddle bag with wide, comfortable shoulder straps and a neat topstitched front pocket will hold all the bits and pieces essential for everyday life. While the carpet bag is perfect for around town or weekend jaunts in the country. Choose a durable fabric that not only looks good but is substantial enough for a bag that needs to hold its shape under pressure. To add strength and a fashionable finish, quilt the fabric before making it into a bag (see page 43).

Saddle bag

Stamp your own style on a flower-strewn shoulder bag with curved seams and a topstitched pocket.

You will need
1¼yd (1m) main fabric, 45" (115cm) wide
1¼yd (1m) lining, 45" (115cm) wide
1¼yd (1m) interlining, 36" (90cm) wide
Matching sewing threads
Paper for patterns

To enlarge the patterns
Using the measurements shown on page 40, draw the paper patterns.

To cut out
From main fabric
1 back
1 front
1 pocket
2 handles
1 gusset
From lining
Cut out the same pieces as for the main fabric, omitting the handles
From interlining
Cut out the same pieces as for the main fabric, but cutting only one handle

To prepare the fabric
Place an interlining piece on the wrong side of each fabric piece, interlining only one handle piece only. Baste, keeping the fabric and interlining pieces flat.

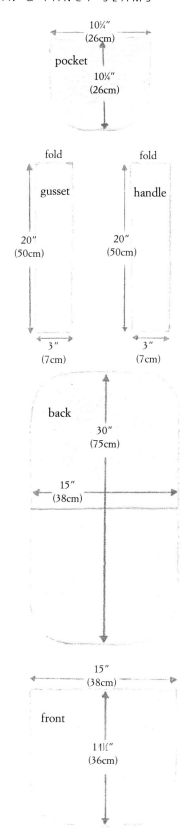

pocket
10¼" (26cm)
10¼" (26cm)

fold · fold
gusset · **handle**
20" (50cm) · 20" (50cm)
3" (7cm) · 3" (7cm)

back
30" (75cm)
15" (38cm)

front
15" (38cm)
14½" (36cm)

To make and attach the pocket

1 With right sides together, pin and baste the pocket lining to the interlined pocket piece. Stitch, leaving a small gap to turn through.

2 Trim the seam allowances, and turn right side out. Slipstitch the gap closed and press. Topstitch across the top of the pocket close to the edge.

3 Position the pocket on the right side of the bag front, 3" (7cm) in from the sides and 3" (7cm) up from the bottom edge (fig 1). Then pin, baste, and topstitch the pocket in place.

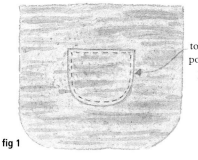

topstitch pocket in place

fig 1

To make the handle

1 Turn under ⅝" (1.5cm) at the short ends of the interlined handle piece and press.

2 With right sides together, join the 2 handle pieces along the long edges.

3 Trim, turn right side out, and press. Topstitch along both long edges.

To complete the bag

1 With right sides facing, join the short ends of the handle to the gusset piece, being careful not to catch the turned-under ends in the stitching.

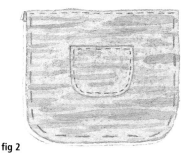

fig 2

To make the front

1 With right sides together, join the front lining to the interlined front piece along the top edge. Press, trim the seam allowances, and turn to the right side.

2 Topstitch along the top edge, then baste the rest of the front lining to the front piece, wrong sides together and raw edges mattching (fig 2).

To make the back

1 With right sides together, place the back lining on the interlined back piece. Pin, baste, and stitch together only around the flap.

2 Trim and clip the seam allowances, clipping into the stitching at the end. Turn to the right side. Press. Topstitch around the flap close to the edge.

3 Lay the rest of the lining over the rest of the back piece, wrong sides together, and baste.

2 With right sides together, join the gusset to the front and back pieces of the bag. The front and back linings should be included in the seams.

3 Turn under ⅝" (1.5cm) at both short ends and along one long edge of the gusset lining and press.

4 Join the unfolded long edge of the gusset lining to the front of the bag so that the gusset lining and the right side of the front lining are facing. The front of the bag will now be sandwiched between the gusset and the gusset lining. Clip, trim, and press the seam allowances toward the gusset.

5 Bring the gusset lining over the gusset and slipstitch the folded long edge of the gusset lining to the machine stitching of the other gusset seam.

6 Stitch the folded short ends of the handle to the short ends of the gusset lining. Turn the bag right side out.

Carpet bag

This classic carpet bag can be made in a strong pile fabric, backed with lining to give added style and stability, or in a strong quilted cotton. Generous-size handles make the bag easy to carry.

You will need
1⅜yd (1.2m) main fabric, 54" (137cm) wide
1⅜yd (1.2m) lining fabric, 54" (137cm) wide
Matching sewing threads
30" (75cm) zipper
Paper for patterns

To enlarge the patterns
Using the measurements shown on page 43, draw the paper patterns.

To cut out
From main fabric
1 bag
2 handles
2 zipper gussets
1 gusset
From lining
Cut out the same pieces as for the main fabric, omitting handles and zipper gussets

To make the handles
1 With right sides together and raw edges matching, fold both handle pieces in half lengthwise. Pin, baste, and stitch along the long edges.
2 Trim the seam allowances, turn both handles right side out, and press. Turn in the ends and slipstitch. Press.

To make the front and back
1 With wrong sides together, place the front and back linings on the main front and back pieces, and baste.
2 Position the handles 4½" (11cm) down from the top edge and 6¾" (17cm) in from the side edges. Stitch a square at each end to secure (fig 1).

To insert the zipper
1 With wrong sides together, fold both zipper gusset pieces in half lengthwise.
2 Fold under ⅝" (1.5cm) along one of the long edges of each piece.
3 Center the folded edges on top of the zipper. Then pin, baste, and stitch the zipper in place (fig 2).

To make and join on the gusset
1 With right sides together, join the gusset pieces along one short end, then press the seam open.
2 With right sides together, join this plain gusset piece to the zipper gusset along the short ends. Press the seams toward the gusset without the zipper.
3 With right sides together, join the gusset to the front and back bag pieces, keeping the folded edges of the zipper gusset out of the way.
4 Clip the seam up to the stitching where the zipper plain gussets meet.

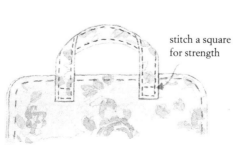

stitch a square for strength

fig 1

fold gusset in half

fig 2

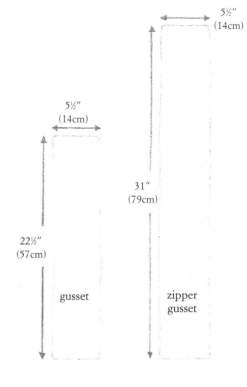

5½"
(14cm)

4"
(10cm)

5½"
(14cm)

31"
(79cm)

23"
(58.5cm)

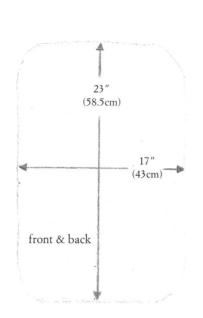

17"
(43cm)

25"
(63.5cm)

22½"
(57cm)

front & back

handle

gusset

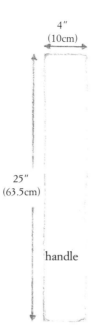

zipper
gusset

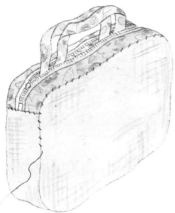

fig 3

To complete the carpet bag

1 Turn under ⅝" (1.5cm) on both short ends of the gusset lining and press.
2 With the right sides of the gusset lining and the front lining facing, sandwich the front piece between the two. Pin, baste, and stitch the gusset lining to the front of the bag. Press the seam toward the gusset. On the zipper gusset, the seam should disappear under the folded edge. Slipstitch the folded edge in place.
3 Bring the gusset lining over the gusset, and slipstitch the long folded edge to the stitching of the other gusset seam with neat stitches (fig 3).
4 Slipstitch the short folded edge to the zipper gusset. Open the zipper and turn the bag right side out.

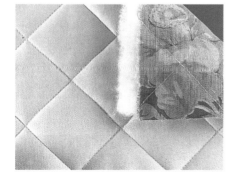

Quilting

Quilting is traditionally used to add warmth to fabrics. Batting is sandwiched between two layers of fabric which are then stitched together, either by hand or machine. The stitching can be be worked either in straight lines or made into a feature following intricate patterns, which look especially effective on plain fabrics.

Quilted fabric is also protective and strong, making it especially suitable for bags. Vertical lines of topstitching can be applied to decorate either bag.

1 Mark evenly spaced lines across the bag about 1"–2" (2.5–5cm) apart.
2 Place the batting between the fabric and the lining. Baste firmly from the center out to the edges.
3 Stitch along the marked lines, using matching or contrasting thread.
4 Measure and mark the horizontal quilting lines and stitch in the same way to complete.

43

bench cushion

Outdoor living is becoming increasingly popular, and a cushioned garden bench makes it much more comfortable. Once the art of gusset making has been mastered, box cushions are not difficult to construct. Choose a strong, durable fabric that can weather the sunlight and light summer showers when stitched around a foam rubber cushion. The extra long zipper will help to ease the cover off the cushion, making it easy to launder.

You will need

Paper for patterns
Fabric (see To cut out, below)
Matching sewing thread
Fabric for piping
Zipper, equal in length to back edge of
    cushion plus 8" (20cm)
Foam rubber cushion of desired size
Paper for patterns

To cut out

1 Measure the cushion, and draw a paper pattern for the top and base sections, adding twice the seam allowance to the length and width.
2 Make a paper pattern for the zipper gusset, the same length as the zipper plus twice the seam allowance, by the depth of the cushion plus twice the seam allowance. Make a paper pattern for the remaining gusset section by measuring the remaining length around the cushion and adding twice the seam allowance all around. It may be necessary to join 2 pieces together to achieve the required length.
3 Prepare the main fabric by straightening the raw edge so that it is at a right angle to the selvages.
4 Place the cushion top pattern piece on the main fabric, making sure that any printed design is centralized and that the long side lies parallel to the newly cut edge of the fabric. Pin in position. Repeat with the base pattern piece.
5 Fit the gusset pattern pieces on the fabric, either on the straight grain or on the bias, depending on the effect desired, but be consistent. Cut out all the pattern pieces. Cut a second zipper gusset piece.

To make and insert the piping

1 From the piping fabric cut ¾" (2cm) wide bias strips and join them together into one length twice the circumference of the cushion, plus extra for joining. Fold the piping lengthwise with wrong sides together, and baste.
2 With raw edges together and starting at the center of the back edge, pin the piping in place around the cushion top. Baste up to the first corner.
3 Using a pair of sharp scissors, clip the piping seam allowance to allow it to turn the corner – the clip will open into a right angle (fig 1).
4 Continue to baste the piping in place, clipping the corners in the same way. At the join, stitch the piping together to fit.
5 Repeat steps 1–4 on the cushion base.

To make the gusset

1 With wrong sides together, fold each zipper gusset in half lengthwise with wrong sides together. Baste the long edges together.
2 Sew the zipper centrally in between the folded edges of each gusset (fig 2).
3 With right sides together, join the gusset pieces to form a ring. Partially open the zipper.

To finish the bench cushion

1 With right sides together, join the gusset to the top (fig 3) and base sections, clipping the gusset seam allowance at the corners – each clip should open into a right angle at each corner. Stitch the gusset in place.
2 Turn the cushion cover right side out, and open the zipper fully. Insert the cushion, and close the zipper.

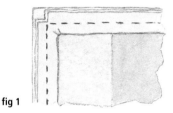

fig 1

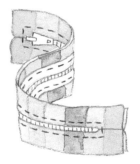

fig 2

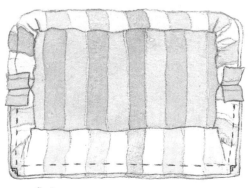

fig 3

wrap-around skirt

This free-flowing skirt made in polyester will pack into a tiny space in a valsie or carryall and come out looking as good as new – a definite must for a holiday wardrobe. The wrap-around style and flattering tie fastening will accommodate all shapes and sizes, and since it's quick to stitch you can easily make several skirts in different fabrics from brightly colored cottons to fine, plain wools.

You will need
2¼yd (2m) polyester fabric, 45" (115cm) wide
Matching sewing thread
Paper for patterns

To enlarge the patterns
Using the measurements shown below, draw the paper patterns. Alternatively, turn to page 98 and enlarge the patterns from the diagrams.

To cut out
1 back
1 left front
1 right front
1 right front facing
1 left front facing
1 back facing
2 ties 33" x 3" (84 x 7cm)

To make the tie
Pin the tie pieces together with right sides facing. Trim one end into a point. Baste and stitch ½" (12mm) from the long raw edges and across the pointed end. Turn right side out. Press.

To finish the skirt
1 Stitch the darts in the back piece, and press them toward the center back.
2 Join the side seams, leaving a 1" (2.5cm) opening ¾" (2cm) from the top edge on the right-hand side seam (fig 1, right). Finish the seams and press open.
3 Join the side seams on the facings, leaving a 1" (2.5cm) opening ¾" (2cm) from the top edge on the right-hand side seam. Press the seams open. Turn in ¼" (6mm) along the bottom edge of the facing, and machine stitch.

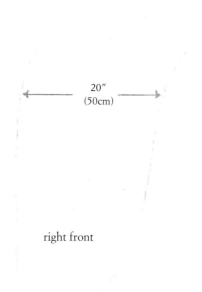

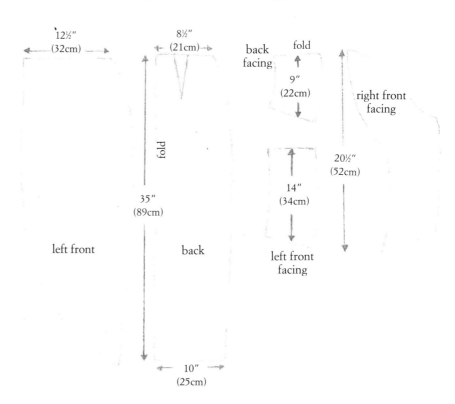

20"
(50cm)

right front

12½"
(32cm)

8½"
(21cm)

fold

35"
(89cm)

left front

10"
(25cm)

back

back facing

fold

9"
(22cm)

14"
(34cm)

left front facing

right front facing

20½"
(52cm)

fig 1

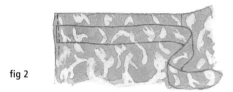

fig 2

fig 3

fig 4

4 With raw edges matching, pin, baste, and stitch the tie in place on the right side of the left-hand front piece (fig 2).
5 With right sides together, pin the facing in position on the skirt, matching the raw edges along the waist, down the front, and around the short tie (fig 3). Match side seams on the skirt and facing.
6 Baste and stitch the facing in place and press. Trim, and clip around the curves.

Turn the facing to the wrong side, and press. Catch facing hem to each seam allowance with a few hand stitches.
7 Match up the gaps left in the skirt and facing seams. Slipstitch the folded edge of the facing seam to the folded edge of skirt seam around the opening (fig 4).
8 Make a ¼" (6mm) hem around the front and along the bottom of the skirt. Slipstitch in place.

47

Gathers, pleats & tucks

Pleats, tucks, darts, gathers, and casings are all designed to reduce fullness in a wide piece of fabric. Skirts and trousers can be full over the hips and, by using one of these methods, can be made to fit neatly around the waist. Curtains can also be made to fit a curtain rod and hang in luxurious folds. Used skillfully and imaginatively, these techniques can add style and interest to a garment or project, as well as being functional. One of the most dramatic ways to pleat the top of a curtain is to use triple pleats, and these are shown to great effect on the door curtain in this chapter. The loose-fitting trousers demonstrate one of the simplest methods of pulling in fullness – with a drawstring casing. In the shirts, the fullness is taken up by the yoke and again at the cuff, while tucks serve a purely decorative role in the jewelry pouch.

Once you have perfected these methods, you can use your new-found skills in a variety of ways on garments and home furnishings.

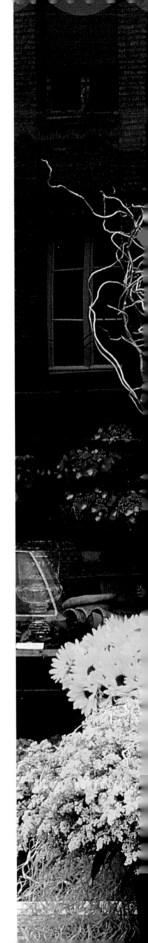

gathers & tucks

Gathering is one of the simplest ways of taking in fullness. Extra fullness is gathered up to the required width by pulling up a running stitch, and this method can be used on skirts at the waist, on sleeves at the head or cuff, on yokes, or to make ruffles. To look professional, gathers must be made with care. They need to be distributed evenly and stroked down individually with a pin to make them lie neatly.

Tucks control fullness in a precise way – each one needs to be accurately measured, pinned, and stitched, to achieve a neat result. Tucks can also be used in a purely decorative way.

Making gathers

Gathering can be done by hand with a simple running stitch, or by machine using a large straight stitch and a loose tension, or by using a ruffler attachment.

By hand

The thread for gathering needs to be strong so that it can be pulled up without breaking.

1 Cut a piece of thread 4" (10cm) longer than the length to be gathered. This may be much longer than you are used to working with, but it is essential not to have joins.

2 Secure the thread. Work two rows of small running stitches approximately ¼" (6mm) apart, one above and one below the seam line (fig 1). The stitches should lie exactly above each other. Avoid gathering over a seam; instead, stop and start again on either side.

3 Do not secure the thread ends but leave them hanging until you are ready to pull them up.

4 Divide the gathered edge into an equal number of sections and mark with pins. Take the flat piece to be joined to the gathers and divide it into matching sections, marking with pins.

5 Place the flat piece of fabric right side up, and position the gathered piece on top with the raw edges matching. Pin the two pieces of fabric together at the marked points. The pins should be placed at right angles to the raw edges and positioned so as not to interfere with pulling up the gathers.

6 Pull up the two gathering threads together until the gathered piece of fabric is the same length as the ungathered piece. Anchor the ends of the threads by twisting them around a pin in a figure-eight motif.

7 Arrange the gathers evenly. Put in more pins, then baste and machine stitch along the seam line.

8 Remove the gathering and basting threads. On the right side, stroke down the gathers with a pin.

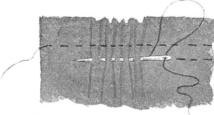

fig 1

By machine

The basic method for making gathers by machine is the same as by hand, apart from the following points:

• Before stitching the two rows of gathering stitches, loosen the upper tension of the machine slightly and select the longest stitch length.

• Pull up the bobbin threads together from both ends (fig 2), and anchor on the pins at both ends.

fig 2

pull up bobbin threads

Casings and drawstrings

A casing is one of the simplest ways in which to control fullness. It consists of a channel made in the fabric through which a piece of elastic, cord, or ribbon is threaded and then pulled up to the required length. Casings have the advantage of being adjustable; they can also be used on curtains, where a rod can be threaded through the casing to gather up the fullness.

Elastic casing

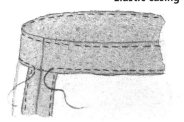

fig 3

An elastic casing is not quite as adjustable as a drawstring, because the elastic is stitched to a fixed length.
1 Fold over the edge of the fabric along the fitting line, and baste the folded edge. Tuck in the raw edge and baste.
2 Stitch along the top of the casing and again along the fold at the lower edge of the casing, leaving a gap in the stitching (fig 3) through which to thread the elastic. Position the gap over a seam.
3 Fasten a safety pin to one end of the elastic, and feed it around the casing. Overlap the ends of the elastic for ¾" (2cm), and stitch the ends together firmly. Stitch the gap closed.

Drawstring casing

A drawstring casing is made in the same way as an elastic casing, but an opening must be left through which the drawstring can emerge. The simplest way to do this is to leave an opening in a seam. The other way is to make eyelets or buttonholes in the casing fabric before the casing itself is formed.

Tucks

Tucks are an attractive way of controlling fullness, but can also be used purely as decoration. They can be made on the right or wrong side of the fabric, but it is more usual for them to show on the right side. In addition, tucks can be stitched along their whole length or only part of the way, releasing the fullness where the stitching stops.

Tucks are usually grouped together; their width, and the spacing between them, can be varied to produce a range of different effects.

Tucks are made on the straight grain of the fabric. The folds and stitching must be exactly parallel, and great care must be taken to insure accuracy.

Pintucks are simply tiny tucks stitched very close to the folds. They can also be made successfully using a specialist sewing machine foot and twin needle.

1 Fold the fabric along the straight grain with wrong sides together.
2 Measure the required width of the tuck from the fold, and baste along this line through both layers of fabric (fig 4), checking the measurement as you go. Measure and baste all the tucks.
3 Stitch all the tucks along the basting lines. The quilting guide on your machine can help to make the stitching lines exactly parallel to the folds. Make sure that you stitch all the tucks from the same side, so that the top thread of the machine is uppermost when the tucks are pressed to one side.
4 Remove the basting. Press the stitching, and then press the tucks to one side (fig 5).

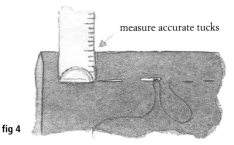

measure accurate tucks

fig 4

fig 5

drawstring trousers

Simple drawstring trousers are extremely comfortable to wear, as the combination of elastic and drawstring ties can be adjusted to fit any size of waist. These are made in sandwash silk, for a look that is both casual and smart. You can make the same pattern in another fabric to create a completely different effect.

You will need
3yd (2.5m) silk, 45" (115cm) wide
Matching sewing thread
1¾yd (1.5m) elastic, ⅜" (1cm) wide
Small square fusible interfacing
Paper for patterns

To enlarge the patterns
Using the measurements shown on the shapes on page 54, draw the patterns. Alternatively, turn to page 100 and enlarge the patterns from the diagrams.

To cut out
2 trouser backs
2 trouser fronts
4 pockets
1 waistband

To attach the pockets and join the outside legs
1 Lay the front leg pieces right side up on a flat surface. Place a pocket piece right side down on top of each leg piece, with the side edges matching and the top edge of the pocket matching the top edge of the leg piece.
2 Pin and baste the edge of the pocket piece to the side edge of the leg piece. Stitch in place ¼" (6mm) from the edge (fig 1). Finish the seam edges, and press the seam allowances toward the pocket. The pocket piece should now stick out at the outside edge of the leg piece (fig 2). Stitch the pocket pieces to the back trouser pieces in the same way.

fig 1

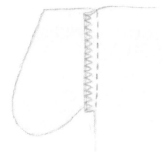

fig 2

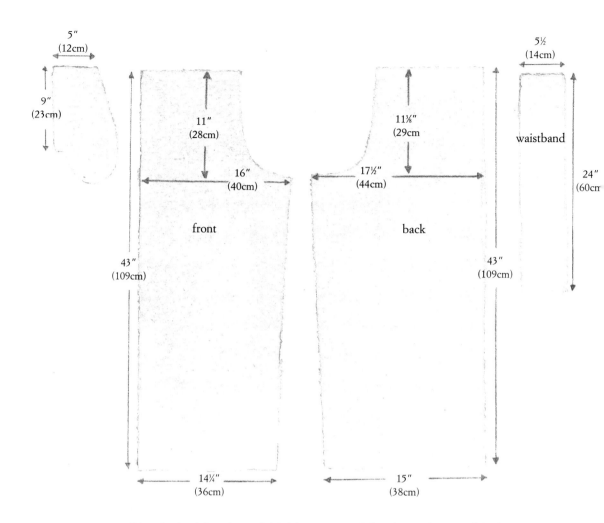

5"
(12cm)

9"
(23cm)

11"
(28cm)

16"
(40cm)

front

43"
(109cm)

14¼"
(36cm)

11⅛"
(29cm)

17½"
(44cm)

back

43"
(109cm)

15"
(38cm)

5½
(14cm)

waistband

24"
(60cm)

3 Lay the back leg pieces right side up on a flat surface. Place the front leg pieces right side down on top of the back leg pieces, matching up the raw edges of the outside legs and the pockets. Pin and baste these pieces together.

4 Starting at the top of the leg seam, stitch each outside leg seam for 2" (5cm). Leave an opening of 6" (15cm), then complete the seam (fig 3).
5 Stitch around the pockets, joining the stitching to side-seam stitching (fig 4).
6 Clip the seam allowance below the pockets to allow you to press it toward the front of the trousers. Finish the seam edges, then baste the upper edge of the pocket to the top of the trousers.

To join the inside legs
1 Match up the raw edges of each inside leg. Pin and baste. **Note:** the back leg pieces are bigger than the fronts and therefore will no longer lie flat.
2 Starting at the top, stitch. Finish these seam edges. Press.

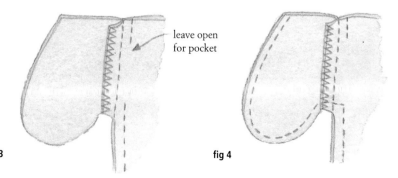

leave open
for pocket

fig 3

fig 4

To join the crotch
1 With right sides facing and the crotch seams matching, place one leg inside the other. Pin and baste the crotch (fig 5).
2 Stitch the crotch seam, and reinforce it with a second row of stitching.
3 Trim the seam on either side of the inside leg seam for about 6" (15cm), and serge or overcast the raw edges together. Clip the seam allowance above this point to allow you to press open the upper part. Finish the seam edges.

To make and join on the waistband
1 Iron a small square of interfacing on the wrong side behind the eyelet positions, and work 2 eyelets or buttonholes by hand or machine (fig 6).
2 Pin and baste the waistband ends together to form a circle. At one side, stitch ⅝" (1.5cm), then leave an opening of 1½" (4cm) and stitch the last ⅝" (1.5cm) (fig 7). Keep the basting in place.

3 With right sides together, place the waistband on the trousers at the waist, matching the waistband seams to the side seams. Pin, baste, and stitch the waistband in place, then press the seam toward the waistband and trim (fig 8).
4 Turn the waistband to the wrong side of the trousers, and turn under the seam allowance on the raw edge. Pin this folded edge to the first line of stitching, and slipstitch in place. Press the waistband, paying particular attention to the folded edge at the top.
5 Make a row of machine stitches ⅝" (1.5cm) down from and parallel to the folded edge of the waistband, then make a second row of stitching 1" (2.5cm) down from and parallel to the other row, to make 3 channels.
6 Remove the earlier basting, and thread elastic through the top and bottom channels (fig 9). Join the elastic, and slipstitch the openings closed.

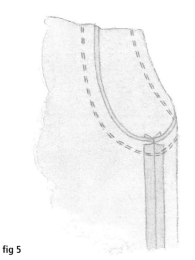

fig 5

fig 6

leave gaps for elastic

fig 7

fig 8

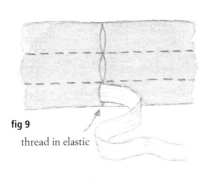

fig 9

thread in elastic

To make the tie
1 Cut a tie strip 80" x 1½" (200 x 4cm). Fold the tie strip in half lengthwise with right sides together, and machine stitch ¼" (6mm) from the long raw edge. Trim. Turn the tie right side out. Tuck in the ends and slipstitch.
2 Thread the tie through the center channel, and knot the ends.

To finish the trousers
Turn up 2" (5cm) hems at the bottom edges of the trouser legs, tuck under the raw edges. Pin, baste, and slipstitch.

55

jewelry pouch

This jewelry pouch makes a delightful gift, and you will want to make one for yourself as well. The fabric used here is striped, and the pieces have been cut to make full use of this effect. However, the pouch is equally successful made in a plain fabric – particularly silk, which catches the light so well. The surface decoration of pintucks makes an attractive finishing touch.

You will need

30" (75cm) fabric, 45" (115cm) wide
Matching sewing thread
16" (40cm) batting, 36" (90cm) wide
Snap

To cut out and prepare the pieces

1 Cut out the following pieces in fabric, adding ½" (12mm) for seam allowances unless otherwise specified:
Front 7½" x 25" (19 x 62.5cm)
Front facing 7½" x 8½" (19 x 21cm)
Back 7½" x 8½" (19 x 21cm)
Back facing 7½" x 8½" (19 x 21cm)
Leaf 11" x 7" (28 x 18cm)
Front pocket 6½" x 5¾" (16.5 x 14.5cm)
Back pocket 8½" x 6¾" (21 x 17cm)
Flap 3½" x 8½" (9 x 21cm)
Ties (2) 11" x 1" (28 x 2.5cm), plus ¼" (6mm) seam allowance
Roll 6" x 2" (15 x 5cm), plus ¼" (6mm) seam allowance
2 Cut out 2 pieces of batting, one 7" x 5½" (18 x 14cm) and the other 14" x 8½" (35 x 21cm).

To make the tucks

1 Make ¼" (6mm) tucks parallel with the long edges across the front piece. Press all the tucks in one direction. From this tucked piece, cut out a rectangle 7½" x 8½" (19 x 21cm).
2 Work a row of stitching parallel to and ⅜" (1cm) away from the edge along and through the tucks in the direction in which they have been pressed. Work another row of stitching 4½" (11cm) from the same edge, keeping the tucks lying in the same direction.
3 Making the tucks lie in the opposite direction, work 2 more parallel rows of stitching, ⅜" (1cm) and 4½" (11cm) away from the opposite edge.
4 Join the front and back pieces along one long side. Trim and press.

To make and attach the pockets

1 Pin and baste a double ½" (12mm) hem at the top of the front pocket piece. Stitch in place. Turn under ½" (12mm) on the remaining 3 sides and press.
2 Place the pocket, right side up, in position on the front facing, an equal distance from each side edge and 1" (2.5cm) from the bottom edge. Pin, baste, and stitch it in position, working a small triangle at either side of the top of the pocket (fig 1).
3 Make a hem along one of the long sides of the back pocket piece in the same way as for the front pocket. Make a similar hem along one of the long sides of the flap piece.
4 Place the pocket piece on top of the back facing with raw edges together. Place the flap on top, with the hem overlapping the pocket hem and the raw edges matching the facing (fig 2). Pin, baste, and stitch together ¼" (6mm) away from the raw edge.

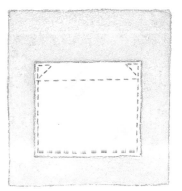

fig 1

fig 2

To make and attach the leaf

1 Fold the leaf piece in half widthwise with right sides together. Place a piece of batting behind, then pin, baste, and stitch along the 2 short edges (fig 3). Trim the seam allowances, then turn right side out, and press.

2 Place the leaf on top of the front facing, with the raw edges matching the raw edges on the right side of the facing and an equal distance from the top and bottom.

3 With right sides together and edges matching, place the back facing (plus pocket) on top of the front facing with the leaf sandwiched in between. Pin, baste, and stitch this one edge together (fig 4). Trim and press.

To make and attach the roll

1 Fold the roll piece in half lengthwise with right sides together, and stitch ¼" (6mm) from the long raw edge and across one end. Turn right side out, and stuff with scraps of batting. Turn in the ends and slipstitch.

2 Stitch one side of a snap to one end of the roll. Place the roll on the front facing between the top of the pocket and the top edge of the facing.

3 Stitch one end of the roll to the facing, then stitch the other half of the snap to the facing to match up with the snap section on the roll.

To make and attach the ties

1 Fold the tie pieces in half lengthwise with right sides together, and stitch ¼" (6mm) from the long raw edge. Turn right side out.

2 Baste the ties in place halfway down the pouch, one on the right and one on the left side of the facing (fig 5).

fig 3

tack tie in the center

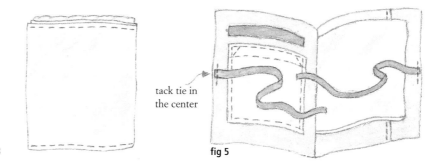

fig 5

fig 4

To finish the jewelry pouch

1 With right sides together, place the front and back pieces on top of the facings, sandwiching the ties in between. Pin and baste in place.

2 Place the batting pieces on top of these pieces, and baste in place. Stitch through all layers ½" (12mm) from the edge all the way around, leaving a gap of about 3" (7cm) for turning. Turn the pouch right side out, and press. Slipstitch the gap closed.

3 Tuck in the raw edges of the ties and slipstitch in place.

shirts

Shirts are always in fashion and make a welcome addition to any wardrobe. These cool shirts are made in linen and plain cotton. The linen version is made very simply with a pleat at the back, and the pattern is then adapted for the lawn shirt, with pintucks added for decoration and gathers replacing the pleat at the back.

Plain shirt

Clean-cut lines and cool linen fabric make this an ideal shirt. The smart, topstitched sleeve openings add to the tailored look. Wear it tucked into trousers or hanging free.

You will need
3yd (2.5m) linen, 45" (115cm) wide *or*
  2¼yd (2m) linen, 60" (150cm) wide
Matching sewing thread
10" (25cm) interfacing, 36" (90cm) wide
11 buttons
Paper for patterns

To enlarge the patterns
Using the measurements shown on the shapes on page 62, draw the patterns. Alternatively, turn to page 102 and enlarge the patterns from the diagrams.

To cut out
From fabric
1 back
2 back yokes
1 left front
1 right front
2 sleeves
2 collars
2 cuffs
2 plackets
From interfacing
1 collar
2 cuffs

To make the pleat
1 Mark the center back. Measure and mark 1" (2.5cm) to either side. With the right side of the back piece facing, fold the marks to the center back.

2 Press and baste the pleat along the seam line (fig 1).

To make the back
1 With right sides together, pin and baste a yoke to the upper edge of back.
2 Place the right side of the second yoke piece (the yoke facing) to the wrong side of the back piece. Pin, baste, and stitch through all layers, sandwiching the back between the 2 yoke pieces (fig 2). Press the seam toward the yoke.
3 Make a double ¼" (6mm) hem on the lower edge of back, and stitch in place.

To make the front
1 On the right front piece, fold the buttonhole band to the right side along the fold lines. Pin, baste, and stitch the band to the right side of the front.
2 On the left front piece, fold the band to the wrong side along the fold lines.
3 With right sides together, pin, baste, and stitch the front edges of the yoke to the upper edge of the fronts. Press the seam allowances toward the yoke.
4 Bring the yoke facing over to the front, turn under the seam allowance, and slipstitch to the machine stitching. Baste the yoke pieces together at the neck and shoulder edge.
5 Make a double ¼" (6mm) hem along the lower edge of the front and stitch.

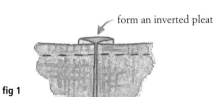

form an inverted pleat

fig 1

sandwich back between yokes

fig 2

fig 3

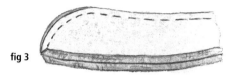

fig 4

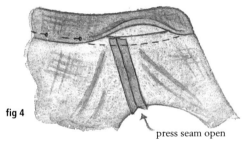

press seam open

fig 5

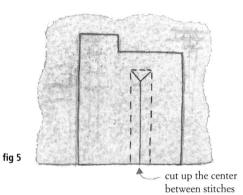

cut up the center
between stitches

fig 6

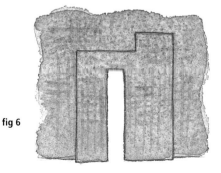

To make and attach the collar

1 Pin and baste the collar interfacing to one collar piece.

2 Turn under the seam allowance along the lower edge of the remaining collar piece. Press, and then trim.

3 With right sides facing, pin, baste, and stitch the collar pieces together, leaving the lower edge open (fig 3). Trim and press. Turn right side out, and press.

4 With right sides together, pin, baste, and stitch the unfolded edge of the collar to the neck edge of the shirt. Press the seam toward the collar. Pin the remaining folded edge of the collar over the previous stitches; pin and baste (fig 4). Topstitch around the collar.

To make and set in the sleeves

1 For each sleeve, turn under a ⅜" (1cm) seam allowance along both the side edges and the short upper edge of the placket and press.

2 Place the right side of the placket on the wrong side of the sleeve, over the marked placket position. Make a rectangle of stitching ¾" x 5" (2 x 12cm), 1½" (4cm) from the shorter edge of the placket. Cut up the center of this rectangle to within ¼" (6mm) of the top, and clip into the corners close to the stitching (fig 5).

3 Turn the placket to the right side of the sleeve, and press the seam allowances toward the placket (fig 6).

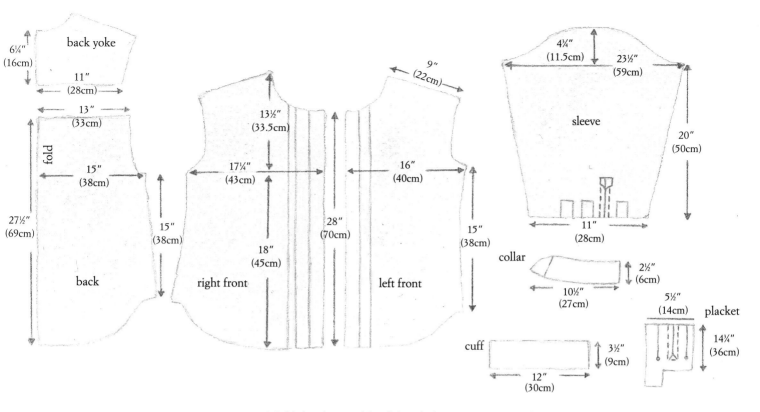

back yoke
6¼" (16cm)
11" (28cm)
13" (33cm)
fold
15" (38cm)
27½" (69cm)
back

13½" (33.5cm)
17¼" (43cm)
15" (38cm)
18" (45cm)
28" (70cm)
right front

9" (22cm)
16" (40cm)
15" (38cm)
left front

4¾" (11.5cm)
23½" (59cm)
sleeve
20" (50cm)
11" (28cm)

collar
2½" (6cm)
10½" (27cm)

cuff
3½" (9cm)
12" (30cm)

5½" (14cm)
placket
14¼" (36cm)

4 Fold the shorter side of the placket in half lengthwise over the seam, and stitch in place (fig 7). Repeat with the longer side of the placket. Pin the upper edge of the placket to the sleeve, and stitch in place (fig 8).

5 Make 3 pleats 1½" (4cm) deep at the lower edge of the sleeve, one on the underside of the sleeve and 2 on the upper, all facing the placket. Baste the pleats in place.

6 With right sides together, pin, baste, and stitch the sleeve to the main body of the shirt. Press the seam allowances toward the shoulder and topstitch.

7 Join the side seam of the main body from the hem through to the lower edge of the sleeve.

To make and attach the cuffs

1 For each cuff, pin and baste the cuff interfacing to the wrong side of the cuff piece. Fold the cuff in half lengthwise, right sides together. Turn up, press, and trim the seam allowance along one long edge of the cuff.

2 Stitch the short ends of the cuff together. Turn right side out. Press.

3 Pin, baste, and stitch the unfolded edge of the cuff to the right side of the sleeve. Trim the seam allowances, and press them toward the cuff.

4 Slipstitch the folded edge of the cuff to the machine stitching on the wrong side. Topstitch around the cuff.

To finish the shirt

Make buttonholes at equal intervals down the front band, and on the cuffs and placket. Sew buttons onto the shirt to correspond with the buttonholes.

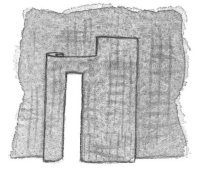

63

Pintucked shirt

fig 1

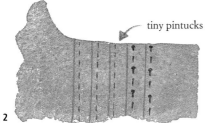

tiny pintucks

fig 2

A good finished result depends on the accuracy of the pintucks. Make sure that they are measured and stitched with care for a professional look.

You will need
3yd (2.5m) cotton lawn, 45" (115cm) wide or 2¼yd (2m) cotton lawn, 60" (150cm) wide
Matching sewing thread
10" (25cm) interfacing, 36" (90cm) wide
11 buttons
Paper for patterns

To enlarge the patterns
Using the measurements shown on the shapes below, draw the patterns. Alternatively, turn to page 102 and enlarge the patterns from the diagrams.

To cut out
From fabric
1 back
2 back yokes
2 fronts
2 sleeves
2 collars
2 cuffs
2 plackets

From interfacing
1 collar
2 cuffs

To make the back
1 Gather the upper edge of the back piece 6" (15cm) in from either side and pull the gathers to match the lower edge of the yoke (fig 1).
2 With right sides together, pin and baste a yoke piece to the gathered upper edge of the back piece.
3 Follow steps 2 and 3 of the back instructions for the Plain Shirt.

To make the front
1 Make 5 pintucks, each ¼" (6mm) wide and ⅜" (1cm) apart, down the front of the shirt, starting 5¼" (13cm) from the edge (fig 2).
2 Follow steps 1–5 of the front instructions for the Plain Shirt.

To finish the shirt
To make and attach the collar, sleeves, cuffs, buttonholes, and buttons, follow the instructions for the Plain Shirt.

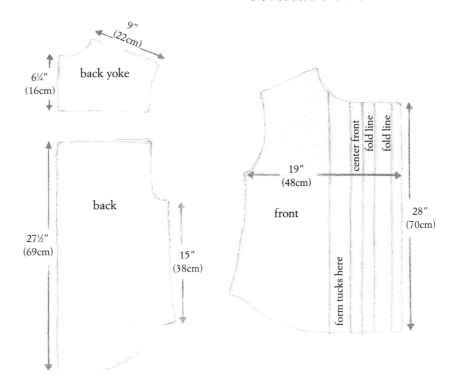

9" (22cm)

6¼" (16cm)

back yoke

back

27½" (69cm)

15" (38cm)

19" (48cm)

center front

fold line

fold line

front

form tucks here

28" (70cm)

pleats

At their simplest, pleats are folds of fabric taken in wherever fullness needs to be controlled. Successful pleats do rely on careful measuring, marking, and stitching.

Pleats are sometimes formed and then attached to another, shorter piece of fabric with a seam. If the pleats are then allowed to fall softly without further stitching, they are called unpressed pleats. For a more structured style, the pleats can be pressed down their full length. To help keep pleats in shape, they can be stitched part of the way down the folds. On curtains, pleats are not normally enclosed in a seam, but are formed on the top finished edge of the curtain and then partially stitched down to keep them in place.

There are several types of pleats including knife, box, and inverted pleats, which are used mainly in garments, and cartridge, goblet, and triple pleats, which are used almost exclusively in curtains and draperies and other soft furnishing projects.

Raised pleats

These pleats do not lie flat but stand away from the fabric. They are not suitable for garment making and are used almost exclusively used for curtain and drapery headings.

Special curtain tapes are available that can be attached to the fabric so that when the cords are pulled, pleats are formed. However, a more satisfactory and elegant finish is achieved by pleating by hand. Although a lot more work and skill is involved, the superior quality of the finished result is definitely worth the extra effort.

To estimate the fabric required for a hand-pleated heading, allow for between two to two and a half times the width of the curtain rod. A length of buckram, a 5" (12cm) deep heavyweight stiffening strip, is enclosed across the top of the curtain before the hand pleats are formed to give them extra body and shape.

Cartridge pleats

Cartridge pleats are small round pleats spaced at regular intervals along the top of a curtain. The cylindrical forms are filled with rolled-up interfacing to help keep the rounded shape.

1 Measure and mark the positions of the pleats. Generally cartridge pleats need about 3½" (9cm) of fabric to form each pleat. Space the pleats about 5" (12cm) apart across the fabric.
2 Fold the pleats along the top edge of the fabric with wrong sides together, making sure that the top edges are lined up and the pleat markings match. Pin the pleats in position.

3 Stitch exactly parallel to the folded edges of the pleats, from the top edge to ⅝" (1.5cm) below the edge of the buckram (fig 1).
4 Form each pleat into a cylinder shape. Cut a piece of interfacing the depth of the pleat and the circumference of the cylinder. Roll up the interfacing and slide into each pleat (fig 2) to help retain the shape of the pleat.

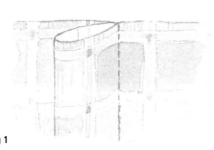

fig 1   fig 2

Goblet pleats

Goblet pleats are made in the same way as cartridge pleats, but they are larger single pleats. The bottom of the pleat is drawn in and secured, and the pleat is stuffed to give a good rounded shape. The finished effect is very grand and elegant, so these pleats are best used on long curtains or draperies where a formal look is required. Once made, curtains with goblet pleats do not draw back easily, so are best left drawn across the window the top and draped open with tiebacks.

1 Measure and mark the positions of the pleats. Generally goblet pleats need 5½" (14cm) to form each pleat. Space the pleats 5½" (14cm) apart.
2 Form the basic pleats as for cartridge pleats, steps 2 and 3 (fig 3).

3 Draw in the base of each pleat tightly and stitch securely with strong thread, molding the upper part of the pleat into a cup or goblet shape (fig 4).
4 Stuff the goblet with padding to give a good rounded shape.

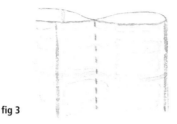

fig 3

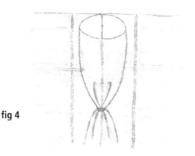

fig 4

Box pleats

Unlike cartridge and goblet pleats, which stand proud, box pleats lie flat. They are suitable for both soft furnishings and garment making, and can be enclosed in a supporting band or formed after the top edge is finished. Sometimes they are allowed to hang freely and loosely, sometimes they are sewn down part of their length for a more formal effect. For tailored pleats, they can be pressed down their full length and held together at their base with a bar tack.

1 Prepare the top edge if necessary. Measure and mark the positions of the pleats. For 2" (5cm) wide pleats, mark 4" (10cm) pleats and 4" (10cm) spaces across the whole curtain top.
2 Form the basic pleats as for cartridge pleats, steps 2 and 3 (fig 5).
3 Fold the pleats flat, with the stitching

line to the center so that there is the same amount of pleat on either side. Press and baste in place (fig 6).
4 If the pleats are to be sewn to a supporting band, stitch the band on now; otherwise, stitch the pleats permanently in position by hand to the depth of the machine stitching.

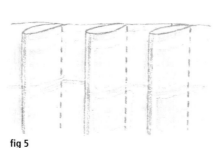

fig 5

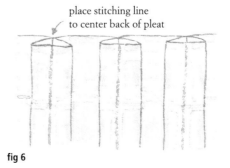

place stitching line to center back of pleat

fig 6

curtain call

Layering a sheer fabric over a heavy linen gives the right thickness for a door curtain without it appearing too heavy and stiff. The bound edge keeps the two fabrics anchored together, while the top is hand stitched with handsome triple pleats. Let the curtain hang straight, with a longer length puddling over the floor, or catch it back to one side in an attractive sweep of fabric.

You will need

Plain linen (see To cut out, below)
Sheer check cotton (see To cut out, below)
Buckram, 5" (12cm) deep, length equal to width of unpleated curtain
Matching sewing threads
Curtain hooks

To cut out

1 Measure the width of the door and add 7" (18cm) for each pleat. Cut out as many widths of linen and of sheer fabric as necessary so that when they are joined they will equal the required width plus 1¼" (3cm).

2 For the top facing, from plain linen cut out the same number of fabric widths as for the main curtain, each 10¼" (26cm) deep.

3 For binding the outer edge, cut out 2 pieces of plain linen each 3½" (9cm) wide, by the curtain length plus 2½" (6cm) for seam allowances; and 1 piece 3½" (9cm) wide, by the curtain width plus 3½" (9cm) for seam allowances.

To make

1 Join the fabric widths together with flat-fell seams to make one piece. Repeat to make one piece in sheer fabric. Lay the linen curtain right side up, then lay the sheer curtain right side up over the linen. Pin and baste the curtains together, matching any seams.

2 Seam the facing lengths together with plain, flat seams. With right sides together and matching seams, place the facing to the top of the curtain, and pin and stitch in place. Trim the seam allowances, then fold down the facing and press with the seam to the edge.

3 Position the buckram between the curtain and the facing. Tuck the bottom edge of the facing up and under the buckram to enclose it, and pin in place.

4 Measure and mark the positions for pleats 7" (18cm) wide, spacing them approximately 5" (12cm) apart, evenly spaced along the top edge of the curtain. Create a triple pleat at each mark.

6 Fold the top edge of the fabric with wrong sides together, making sure that the top edges are lined up and that the pleat markings match. Pin the pleats in position.

7 Stitch exactly parallel to the folded edges of the pleats, from the top edge to ⅝" (1.5cm) below the edge of the buckram (fig 1).

8 Take hold of a pleat between your finger and thumb at the folded edge and push it back to the line of stitching. Another 2 pleats should stick out at either side of your finger and thumb; these 3 pleats should be the same size. Crease these 3 pleats along their length.

9 Overcast neatly across the bottom of each pleat, then overcast at the top of the pleat where the folds meet the machine stitching (fig 2).

fig 1

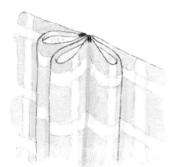

fig 2

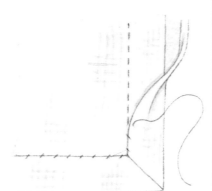

fig 3

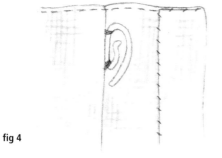

fig 4

To make and attach the binding

1 Fold the binding in half lengthwise with wrong sides facing and press. At one end of each side binding, fold up the raw edges to match the folded edge and press. Unfold and cut along the pressed line. Repeat to cut diagonally across both ends of the base binding.
2 With the binding unfolded, place the mitered edges with right sides facing; pin, baste, and stitch them together to within ⅝" (1.5cm) of the raw edges. Trim and press the seams to edge. Refold the binding in half and press.
3 Place one end of the binding to the outer edge of the curtain with right sides together, matching the mitered seams to the base corners of the curtain. Pin, baste, and stitch the binding to the curtain. At the base corners the binding will fan out to create a neat corner.
4 Tuck under the remaining raw edge of the binding on the wrong side of the curtain, and then slipstitch it by hand to the previous stitches on the wrong side (fig 3). Press.

To finish the curtain

1 At the top edge, tuck under the raw edges of the binding to match the top edge of the curtain, and slipstitch in place as before.
2 Hand sew curtain hooks to wrong side of the curtain, 1½" (4cm) down from top edge. Then sew a hook behind each pleat position (fig 4).
3 Give the curtain a final press, and hang from a curtain rod.

Finishes, fastenings & edgings

Using unusual trimmings adds the final flourish to your sewing projects. Whether you weave fantasies with tassels and fringes or add a sophisticated bound edge, it is clever details that lift the homemade into the world of the professional sewer.

Decorative trimmings emphasize exuberant fabrics and provide a rich contribution to the presentation of your sewing skills. On these pages you will discover how to add a creative touch with confidence and imagination. Choose inventive ways to fasten pillows and clothes, bring a touch of pompon fun to colorful valances, and twist and turn tape into intricate flower designs.

rouleau strips

Rouleau is a narrow tube made from a strip of fabric cut out on the bias, seamed, and turned right side out. It can vary in thickness according to its use and the chosen fabric. The rouleau can either be made flat by trimming down the seam allowances, or fat and round by leaving the seam allowances to add bulk inside the tubing.

Once made, rouleau has many uses. It can make shoestring straps for camisoles and lingerie, can be braided together as an attractive trimming, and may be used as ties and decorative bows, but its most popular use is for button loops. If you are making a lot of rouleau it is worth buying a rouleau turner, which makes life a lot easier.

Making rouleau

For a firm rounded tube, rouleau is padded with its own seam allowance, which instead of being trimmed off is turned to the inside.

1 Cut out a strip of fabric on the bias, to the finished length and four times the finished width required.
2 With right sides together, fold the tube in half lengthwise. Stitch down the strip, stretching the fabric as you go.
3 If you have a rouleau turner, use it to turn the tube right side out. If not, tie the threads from the machine stitching to a large-eyed blunt-ended needle (fig 1), and use this to pull the tube right side out (fig 2).

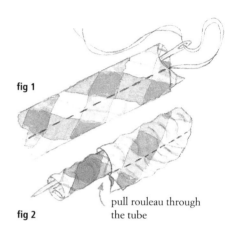

fig 1

fig 2

pull rouleau through the tube

Corded rouleau

Rouleau is much stronger and rounder if it is filled with a cord. Any width of fine cord or piping filler cord can be used. If the fabric is very fine, it is best to use it double or line it with another fabric so that the ridges of the cord are not so prominent.

1 To begin, cut out a narrow strip of fabric on the bias in the same way as for rouleau, above.
2 Cut a piece of cord of the desired thickness and twice as long as the rouleau. Find the center of the cord and place it on the right side of the end of the fabric strip.

3 Fold the fabric strip around the cord, stitch across the end of the strip through the cord to anchor the strip (fig 3), and secure it by stitching close to the cord using the zipper or piping foot.
4 Pull the fabric tube back over the other half of the cord (fig 4), and cut off the excess cord.

fig 3

fig 4

Button loops

Button loops extending beyond the fabric opening make an attractive alternative to buttonholes. Tiny loops look delicate on fine fabrics for lingerie or evening wear, while larger loops can be used on jackets or to fasten pillow covers. The loops can vary greatly in thickness and size depending on their use and the fabric and the design of the article, and may be either hidden or on display. Loops can be made from rouleau, corded rouleau, cord, or fine tape or braid.

A single loop

A single loop can be used on a tailored jacket in place of a buttonhole, and is generally bigger and thicker than the loops in a row. A single loop is usually attached to an edge without the need for a paper guide. Position and sew the single loop in place, and finish the edge with a facing.

1 Make a short length of rouleau. Form it into a single loop, and pin to the right side of the item at the marked position (fig 5) with the ends aligned with the raw edge and the loop facing inward.
2 Stitch along the seam line, and then attach the facing.

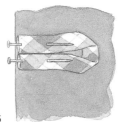

fig 5

Row of loops

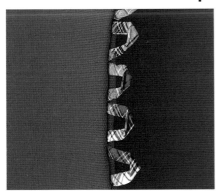

A row of loops fitted together down the front or back of the bodice of a ballgown or wedding dress, with self-covered ball buttons, looks very attractive. Alternatively, space out the loops or group them in twos or threes with a space between the groups. They are also very pleasing on a wide cuff or cummerbund.

1 Make a very narrow rouleau, about three times as long as the opening along which the row of loops will fit.
2 Mark the size and spacing of the loops on a piece of stiff paper the same length as the opening. Mark in the seam line.
3 Pin the rouleau to the paper, and then stitch through the rouleau and the paper, along the seam line (fig 6).

4 Place the paper with the rouleau in position on the right side of the fabric with the rouleau uppermost. Match the seam lines.
5 Stitch the paper and rouleau onto the fabric on top of the first row of stitching, following the marked lines (fig 7). Then tear away the paper. Finish the edge with a facing (fig 8).

fig 6

fig 7

fig 8

75

finishing

A very narrow hand-rolled hem is the most professional way to finish the edge of very fine fabrics such as fine silks, chiffon, and georgette, and is certainly the best choice for the edges of a silk scarf.

Binding is another neat way of finishing an edge. The binding can match the fabric or contrast with it, and the width may vary from very narrow to quite wide, depending on the project and the fabric being used.

Rolled hem

This is quite a difficult process to master, but with a little time and patience it can be done, and the result, although time consuming, is well worth the effort. If you have difficulty in getting the roll started, it is sometimes helpful to make a row of machine stitching near the edge of the fabric and then trim close to it. This gives stability to the edge and makes the rolling easier.

1 Cut a neat edge on the fabric. If it frays easily, it is advisable to trim as you sew.
2 With the wrong side of the fabric facing, use the finger and thumb of your left hand to roll a tiny hem toward you. This may take a little practice.
3 Thread a needle with good-quality silk thread, and pick up a thread under the roll and then another one on the main fabric (fig 1).

4 Continue in this manner, rolling the fabric with the left hand and stitching with the right.

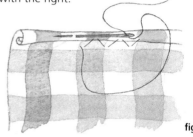

fig 1

Bound edge

The color and width of a bound edge can be chosen to suit an individual project perfectly. For example, silk underwear would require a very narrow binding, probably in a matching color, while at the opposite end of the spectrum, a quilted bedspread would need quite a wide binding, probably in a contrasting color.

If the edge to be bound is completely straight, the binding can be cut on the straight grain of the fabric, but if there are curves, cut the binding on the bias.

1 Cut out the fabric strips for the binding on either the straight grain of the fabric or the bias of the fabric, and to the length required. The width of the binding strips should be twice the required finished width plus two seam allowances.
2 Place the edge of the binding against the edge of the fabric, with right sides

together. Pin, baste, and stitch the binding in place (fig 2).
3 Fold the binding over the edge to the wrong side of the fabric. Turn under the raw edge of the binding, and abutt this fold up to the machine stitching. Pin and baste in position.
4 Slipstitch into the machine stitches, and remove the basting (fig 3). Press.

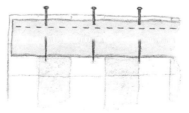

fig 2

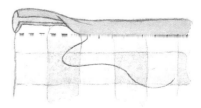

fig 3

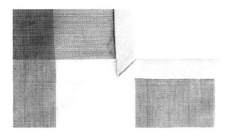

Inside corners

1 Reinforce and clip the corner.
2 With right sides together, stitch the binding to the edge of the fabric, pivoting on the machine needle at the corner and continuing to the end (fig 4).

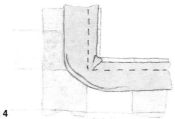

fig 4

3 Make a miter in the binding on the right side, then turn over the work and repeat on the other side.
4 Slipstitch the binding in place on the wrong side onto the machine stitching, then stitch the miters in place (fig 5).

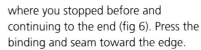

fig 5

Outside corners

1 With right sides together, stitch the binding to the edge of the fabric up to the corner. Remove the work from the sewing machine.
2 Fold the binding back on itself to allow it to bend around the corner, thereby forming a pleat in the binding. Stitch, starting again at the corner at the point

where you stopped before and continuing to the end (fig 6). Press the binding and seam toward the edge.
3 Fold the binding over the edge to the wrong side of the fabric. Turn under the raw edge of the binding, and slipstitch in place onto the machine stitching.
4 Form miters at the corners and slipstitch them in place (fig 7).

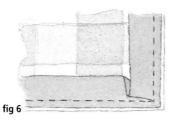

fig 6

fig 7

Six-way binding

A six-way binding is a very attractive and neat way to finish off the edges of garments. As there are six thicknesses of fabric involved, the fabric chosen for the binding should be very fine and soft. This is an ideal way of finishing the neck edge of a collarless blouse or the armhole edge on a sleeveless top.

1 Cut out a binding strip on the bias of the fabric. The strip should be six times the desired width of the finished binding.
2 Fold the strip in half lengthwise with wrong sides together and press lightly.
3 Trim the seam allowance on the garment to slightly less than the finished width of the binding.
4 With right sides facing, line up the raw edges of the binding with the edge of the fabric; pin and baste in position.
5 Stitch along the seam line.

6 Turn the strip over the raw edge to the wrong side of the garment to form a neat folded edge. Slipstitch to the machine stitching of the seam (fig 8).

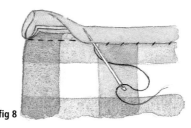

fig 8

trimmings

Trimmings can liven up some of the simplest designs and make them more exciting and interesting. Notions departments are brimming with trimmings of all kinds: ribbons, laces, broderie Anglaise, fringes, tassels, tapes, and many more. You can also make several different trimmings yourself, so that they will match your sewing needs exactly.

Cords

Cords have many applications. They can be used on their own with a tassel on the end, as a pull for window shades or light switches; they make an attractive finish to the edge of pillows; and, looped on curtain headings, they add a finishing touch. There are a lot of cords on the market in various colors and thicknesses, but these are not always exactly right for a particular project. By making your own, you have a much better chance of a good match. There are several different cords that can be made.

Twisted cord

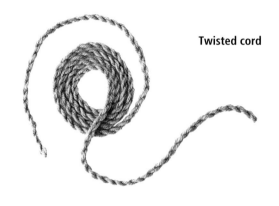

A twisted cord is the easiest type to make. The thickness and texture can be altered by using different threads.

1 Cut as many strands of threads as are needed to make the desired thickness of cord, each three times the finished length you require.

2 Knot the strands together at both ends and loop one end over a hook or door knob. Stretch the cord tightly, and place a pencil between the strands at the opposite end.

3 Holding the pencil close to the knots and keeping the strands taut, revolve the pencil clockwise (fig 1), until the strands are twisted tightly together along their whole length.

4 Keeping the cord taut, grip the center of the twisted strands and walk to meet the other end. Take hold of this end, holding the two knots in one hand and the folded end in the other (fig 2).

5 Now let the folded end go. The cord will form its own twist (fig 3). Tie the knotted ends together firmly.

revolve pencil

fig 1

fold in half

fig 2

fig 3

Finger cord

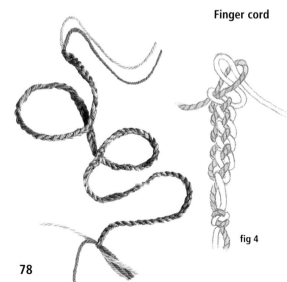

A finger cord is a hand knotted cord consisting of a chain of loops. You slot the loops of thread into each other in turn, or use your fingers instead of hooks to pull through the loops. The process requires a little thought and practice, but is then quite simple to do and effective when finished. Two threads of the same or contrasting colors may be used.

1 Knot two pieces of thread together at one end. Take hold of the knot between the thumb and second finger of your right hand.

2 Loop strand the left-hand thread over your index finger, then keep hold of the end of this strand with your third and fourth fingers.

3 With your left hand, insert the index finger into the loop and bring through the opposite strand, then hold the end of this strand with the third and fourth fingers of your left hand.

4 Now take hold of the knot with your left hand, and release the loop held by your right index finger, pulling the thread tightly to form the cord.

5 Repeat steps 2–4 until the cord is the desired length (fig 4).

fig 4

Ribbon work

Ribbon work is a very simple but effective method of trimming. Because the ribbon or tape is woven, it has selvages that will not fray and can be sewn onto the basic fabric in a single thickness. Part of its attraction is derived from the fact that it is not on the bias and therefore resists turning curves and will not lie down smoothly – as bias tape would – producing a curling-up and textured effect.

1 Mark a design on tissue paper. The design should be basic and very free. Pin the tissue-paper design over the marked positions on the fabric.

2 Carefully pin the ribbon in position over the marked tissue-paper design, inserting the pins at right angles to the ribbon. Allow plenty of ribbon to go around the curves.
3 Baste the ribbon in position. Sew carefully along both sides of the ribbon, using either a straight stitch or small zigzag stitch.
4 Wherever the ribbon needs to be cut, turn under the raw edges and tuck in the corners to give a tidy finish, and stitch over. When all the design has been stitched, tear away the tissue paper.
　A different effect is obtained when the ribbon is sewn on using only one line of stitching down the center of the ribbon (fig 5), allowing it to curl over at the edges.

stitch down
centre of ribbon

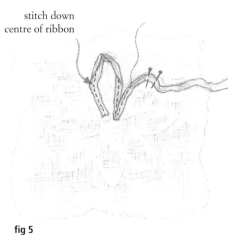

fig 5

Adding a flat trim

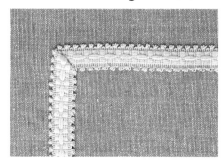

Braid, ribbon, and tape can be topstitched to fabric quickly, either to decorate a pillow cover or to go around a tablecloth or napkin. Neat mitered corners are essential for a professional finish.

1 Pin and baste the trimming right side up along the first edge up to the corner. Stitch along the outer edge.
2 Fold the trim straight back over the stitched length, with the fold matching the fabric edge. Stitch diagonally across the trimming from the corner point, and

trim off the excess (fig 6).
3 Fold back the trimming along the next edge. Repeat, stitching each corner diagonally in the same way. Then join the trimming together to fit. Finally, stitch along the inner edge of the trimming (fig 7).

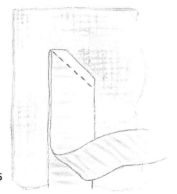

fig 6

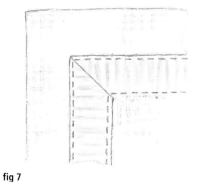

fig 7

fringe

Fringe is an attractive edging, which can be made either from the threads of the main fabric or as a separate trimming. Tassels and pompons also provide a decorative, fringed trimming. All are quick to make from a variey of colorful yarns and threads.

Self fringe

This is made by removing either the weft or warp threads at the edge of a piece of fabric. Not all fabrics are suitable for this treatment: wool or linen fabrics with an even weave are the best types to use, but it is always wise to test out the process on a spare piece of fabric first. A fine wool scarf can be made quickly using this method.

1 Make sure that the edge of the fabric is cut absolutely straight.
2 Decide how long the fringe should be, and make a row of machine stitches along this line to prevent the fringe from growing longer than you want.

3 Using a pin, carefully remove the threads that lie parallel to this row of stitching, starting at the edge of the fabric and working inward until you reach the stitching line. Press the fringe to remove any wrinkles.

Ready-made fringe

A ready-made fringe will often have a decorative top edge that is meant to be seen. Simply hand stitch the fringe on top of the outside edge of the fabric. You may need to work two rows of stitching. Alternatively, the fringe can be sandwiched into a seam and stitched in place when the seam is completed. At the ends, turn in the fringe securely to prevent it from unraveling.

Knotted fringe

Knotted fringes can be made using all kinds of threads and yarns. Wool, silk, cotton, and rayon are all suitable, but for the best results you should match the thread to the fabric in both type and weight.

1 Cut out a cardboard strip to the depth of the intended fringe. Wrap the thread around the cardboard.
2 Use sharp scissors to cut through a few strands of the thread (fig 1).

3 Take a fine crochet hook and poke it through the fabric. Pick up a few strands of thread and fold them in half over the hook (fig 2), then pull them a little way through the fabric using the hook. With the hook still through the loop of threads, pick up the cut ends of the threads and pull them through the loop (fig 3). Pull the knot tight.
4 Continue in this way along the length of the fabric edge, using the same number of threads each time (fig 4). With thick threads, it may be easier to use one thread at a time.

A second set of knots can be made by knotting half the strands from one knot with half the strands from the adjacent knot. On a long fringe this can be repeated several times. Extra thread will be needed to allow for the extra knots, so make up a test piece before calculating the length of thread required.

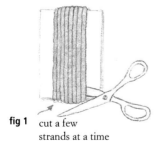

fig 1   cut a few strands at a time

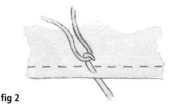

fig 2

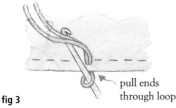

fig 3   pull ends through loop

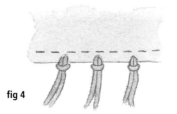

fig 4

Tassels

Tassels are a popular trimming. They can be used in a variety of decorative ways. Individually, they may be used as pulls for window shades or zippers, or on the corners of pillows. Joined in a row, they can make an attractive fringe.

1 Wind a length of thread around two pieces of thin cardboard that are the same depth as that of the required tassel. If making more than one tassel, count the number of "winds" so that all the tassels will be the same size.
2 Thread a tapestry needle with a very long thread and work a line of backstitch a short way down from the top of the wound threads.

3 Hold the top of the cardboard tightly and cut the threads along the base edge (fig 5). Remove the cardboard and you will be left with a skirt of threads.
4 If joining to a cord, wrap the skirt around the knot in the cord, which can be padded to make it larger.
5 Stitch through the skirt top and the knot several times. Wrap a thread around the tassel several times, about one-third of the way down below the knot.
6 Thread a blunt needle with either matching or contrasting thread, work a row of blanket stitch loosely around the "head" of the tassel. Now work a second row of blanket stitches into the loops of the first row.
7 Continue working blanket stitch around the head (fig 6), loosening and tightening the stitches as necessary to keep the rounded shape. Fasten off when the tassel head has been covered.

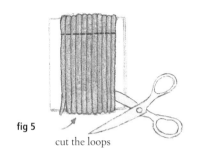

fig 5
cut the loops

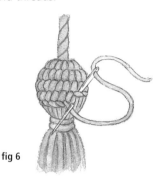

fig 6

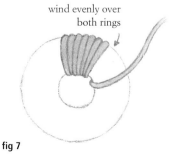

Pompons

Pompons are purely decorative and are great fun. Like tassels, they can be used as pulls at the bottom of a window shade or for a light switch. They can be made from most knitting yarns or embroidery threads. Children love making pompons, and they provide an enjoyable occupation for rainy days.

If making several pompons that need to be the same size, you should count the number of "winds" around the cardboard rings and repeat this number. You must also keep the tension of the thread the same, as a looser tension makes a bigger pompon.

1 Cut out two circles of strong cardboard to the required size. Cut out a smaller circle from the center of each one, about one-quarter the size of the original circle.

2 Put the cardboard rings on top of each other and wind the thread around them, threading it through the central hole (fig 7). Continue until the hole is filled.
3 Insert one blade of a sharp pair of scissors between the cardboard rings, and cut through the threads around the outside edge (fig 8).
4 Take another length of thread and place it around the strands between the cardboard rings. Tie it very tightly and knot, leaving the ends long enough for attaching the pompon.
5 Remove the cardboard rings and shake the pompon. Trim off any untidy ends.

wind evenly over both rings

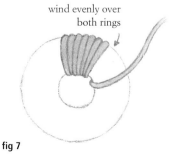

fig 7

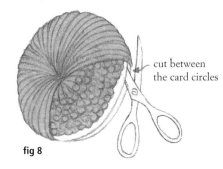

cut between the card circles

fig 8

summer scarves

Scarves do not have to be limited to winter. They can be used as a fashion statement in the summer, too, using fine, light fabrics in soft colors. The first scarf, with its useful pockets, is functional as well as pretty, and uses an interesting combination of linen and silk chiffon. The self fringe makes a pleasing finishing touch. Our long, sheer scarf is made in two colors of silk chiffon.

Pocketed scarf

You will need
32" (80cm) linen fabric, 60" (150cm) wide
32" (80cm) of chiffon, 60" (150cm) wide
Matching sewing threads

To cut out
1 Cut out 2 pieces of linen and 2 pieces of chiffon, each 12" x 45" (30 x 115cm).
2 Cut out 2 strips of linen 12" x 1½" (30 x 4cm).

To make
1 With right sides together, join the 2 pieces of linen along the short edges. Join the 2 pieces of chiffon in the same way. Press both seams.
2 On each of the linen strips, make a row of small zigzag stitches 1" (2.5cm) in from the long edge. Fringe below the line of stitching.
3 With right sides together, place a strip of fringe along one short end of the joined linen and stitch in place ⅝" (1.5cm) from the edge (fig 1). Repeat at the other end.
4 With right sides together, place the joined chiffon on top of the linen. Pin, baste, and stitch in place with a ⅝" (1.5cm) seam allowance, leaving a small gap for turning. Trim the seam allowance, finish the edge, and press.
5 Turn the scarf right side out, and slipstitch the gap closed. Press. Turn down 1" (2.5cm) on each of the short sides, and press.
6 Fold the short ends onto the linen side by 8" (20cm) to form a pocket. Hand or machine stitch along the sides (fig 2).

add self-fringe →

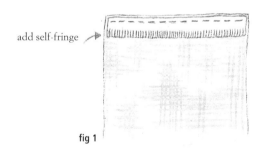

fig 1

fold up to form pockets

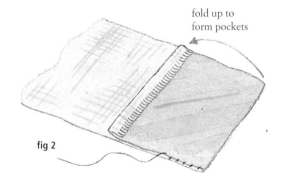

fig 2

Sheer scarf

You will need
18" (45cm) silk chiffon, 60" (150cm) wide
18" (45cm) contrasting silk chiffon, 60" (150cm) wide
Matching sewing threads

To make
1 With right sides and raw edges together, pin and baste the 2 pieces of silk fabric one on top of the other.
2 Stitch around all 4 sides, leaving a small opening on one short side, for turning. Trim the seam allowances and finish the raw edges if necessary. Press.
3 Turn the scarf right side out. Turn in the opening and slipstitch closed.

Alternatively, cut a single length of fabric and simply finish with a hand-rolled hem.

winter scarves

Scarves need not always be long and flowing. These two neat little scarves, suitable for both men and women, use very small amounts of fabric and are cozy and smart. The necktie combines panne and crushed velvet, while our collar scarf is made in wool velour.

Necktie

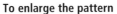

buttonhole

5¼" (13cm)

16" (40cm)

You will need
¾yd (50cm) each of panne velvet and crushed velvet, 45" (115cm) wide
Matching sewing thread
Paper for pattern

To enlarge the pattern
Using the measurements shown on the shape left, draw the paper pattern.

To cut out
From panne velvet
2 shapes
From crushed velvet
2 shapes

To make
1 With right sides together, pin, baste, and stitch the short end of one panne piece to the short end of one crushed velvet piece, and press the seam open.
2 Pin and baste the same seam on the other 2 pieces of fabric. Stitch, leaving a 2" (5cm) gap in the middle for turning (fig 1, right). Press the seam open.
3 With right sides facing, place the 2 pieces together, with different fabrics facing. Pin, baste, stitch all around (fig 2, right), and trim.
4 Turn right side out through the gap in the short seam. Roll the edges between finger and thumb to make sure that the seam comes right to the edge, and press. Join the gap by hand.

To finish the necktie
Make a buttonhole 2" (5cm) long centrally in the necktie, 2½" (6cm) in from one end (fig 3).

Collar scarf

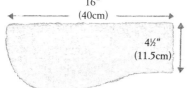

16" (40cm)

4½" (11.5cm)

You will need
16" x 12" (40 x 30cm) wool velour
16" x 12" (40 x 30cm) silk, for lining
Matching sewing thread
1 button
Paper for pattern

To enlarge the pattern
Using the measurements shown on the left, draw the paper pattern.

To cut out
From main fabric
2 shapes
From lining
2 shapes
1 strip 4" x ¾" (10 x 2cm) on the bias

To make
1 Make the rouleau from the lining strip. Baste the rouleau to the fabric 2½" (6cm) along one long straight edge.
2 Join one short end of a main fabric piece to the short end of the other main fabric piece. Trim 1¼" (3cm) off the straight edge of the lining, and then join the corresponding seams.
3 With right sides together, pin, baste, and machine stitch the lining fabric to the main fabric along the long straight edge, catching in the rouleau.
4 Match the raw edges of the curved side of the lining to the raw edges of the curved side of the main fabric; there will be a small margin of fabric on the wrong side. Pin, baste, and machine stitch around the seam, leaving a small gap for turning. Trim the seam allowances.
5 Turn to the right side and pull the curved seam over to the edge. This will bring the top fabric around to the back along the straight edge. Slipstitch the gap. Press.

To finish the scarf
Sew a button to the left-hand side to correspond with the loop, making sure that the edges of the scarf line up.

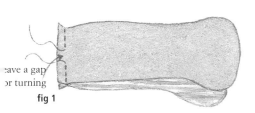

Leave a gap
for turning
fig 1

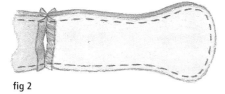

fig 2

fig 3

valance

This jolly valance with its trimming of pompons would brighten up any room, particularly one for a child. Choose a brightly colored fabric with a pattern that lends itself to this design. Measure the length of the valance and divide by the chosen size of the triangular points, so that they will fit exactly across the length. The valance shown is approximately 22" (55cm) deep.

You will need

Fabric to desired width of valance plus twice the seam allowance, by desired depth plus 4½" (11.5cm) for turnings (2 widths of fabric may be required)

Matching sewing thread

Lining fabric to same measurements as main fabric

Thin cardboard for template

Yarn in a variety of colors, for pompons

To cut out and prepare the fabric

Straighten up the main fabric and the lining. Cut out the fabric and lining to the required length. Join the widths with plain flat seams if necessary, pressing the seams open.

To make

1 Place the lining on the table right side up and lay the main fabric over it, wrong side up and with raw edges matching.

2 Decide what size you want the points, and make a template of one point in thin cardboard. Try to make the points fit in with the fabric design if possible; you may need to adjust the width of the valance at this stage so that the points fit across it exactly.

3 On the wrong side of the fabric; work across the width of the valance, drawing around the template for all the points. Baste together the main fabric and lining close to this line. Stitch along the line and up the side edges of the valance. Press.

4 Cut away the fabric below the points, leaving ¼" (6mm) for turning (fig 1). Clip into the angles. Turn the valance right side out, and press.

5 Baste along the top edge through the lining and main fabric to hold them together. Turn in 4" (10cm) and baste along the fold line. Turn under the raw edge by ⅝" (1.5cm), then pin, baste, and stitch along this line (fig 2).

To finish the valance

1 Make pompons following the instructions on page 81, and stitch to the points of the valance, alternating the different colors (fig 3).

2 Hang threaded on a rod or attached with clips on curtain rings.

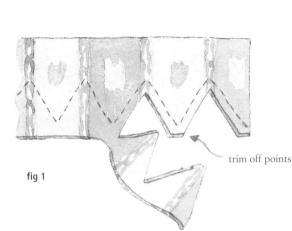

fig 1

trim off points

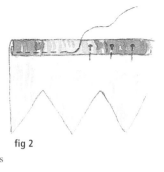

fig 2

fig 3

stitch a pompon to each point

jacket

A loose-fitting jacket – this one with a a generous bound edge – is a useful addition to any wardrobe, and by choosing different fabrics the same pattern can be made appropriate for day or evening wear.

You will need
3yd (2.7m) fabric, 45" (115cm) wide
Matching sewing thread
1½yd (1.2m) interfacing, 36" (90cm) wide
bias binding (optional)
Paper for patterns

To enlarge the pattern
Using the measurements shown on the shapes below, draw the paper patterns. Alternatively, turn to page 104 and enlarge the patterns from the diagrams.

To cut out
From fabric
1 pair fronts
1 back
2 sleeves
2 pockets
2 front bands
2 front band facings
From interfacing
2 front bands

To make and attach the pockets
1 Finish the top edge of each pocket piece by serging, or by turning under the raw edge and stitching.
2 Turn over 1" (2.5cm) at the top of the pocket to the right side. Stitch down the sides of this fold on the seam line (fig 1). Trim and press.
3 Turn the pocket to the wrong side, and turn in the seam allowance on the 3 raw edges, mitering the corners. Baste.
4 Place each pocket on a jacket front piece 2½" (6cm) in from the side edge and 3½" (9cm) up from the bottom edge. Pin, baste, and stitch the pocket in position.

It may help to interface the top fold of the pocket to give it a little more body. You could also stitch the fold down so that it is visible from the right side. Slipstitch the pockets to the front of the jacket if you do not like to see the machine stitching that holds the pockets in place on the right side.

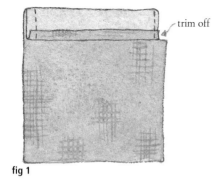

trim off

fig 1

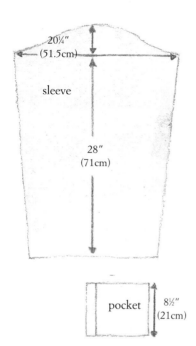

sleeve

20¼" (51.5cm)

28" (71cm)

pocket — 8½" (21cm)

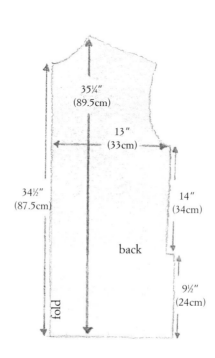

35¼" (89.5cm)

13" (33cm)

34½" (87.5cm)

14" (34cm)

back

fold

9½" (24cm)

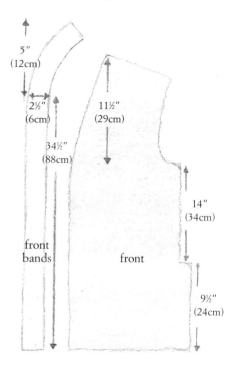

5" (12cm)

2½" (6cm)

11½" (29cm)

34½" (88cm)

14" (34cm)

front bands

front

9½" (24cm)

To attach the front band

1 Pin, baste, and stitch the shoulder seams of the jacket (fig 2).

2 With right sides together, pin the interfacing to the front bands. Join the front bands at center back (fig 3). Join the front band facings at center back.

3 Pin, baste, and stitch the facing to the front band.

4 With right sides together, pin, baste, and stitch the front band to the jacket, along the front and around the neck edge. Turn the facing to the wrong side, and slipstitch in place onto the machine stitching, leaving the bottom few inches (centimeters) free (fig 4).

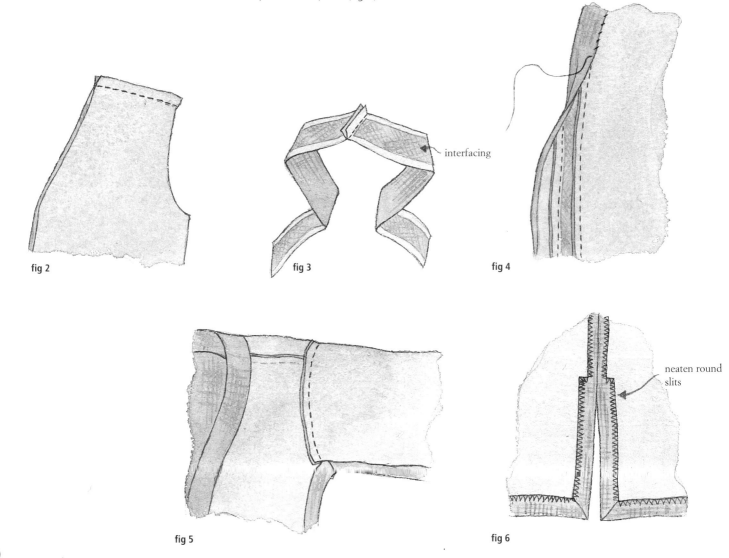

fig 2

fig 3

interfacing

fig 4

fig 5

fig 6

neaten round slits

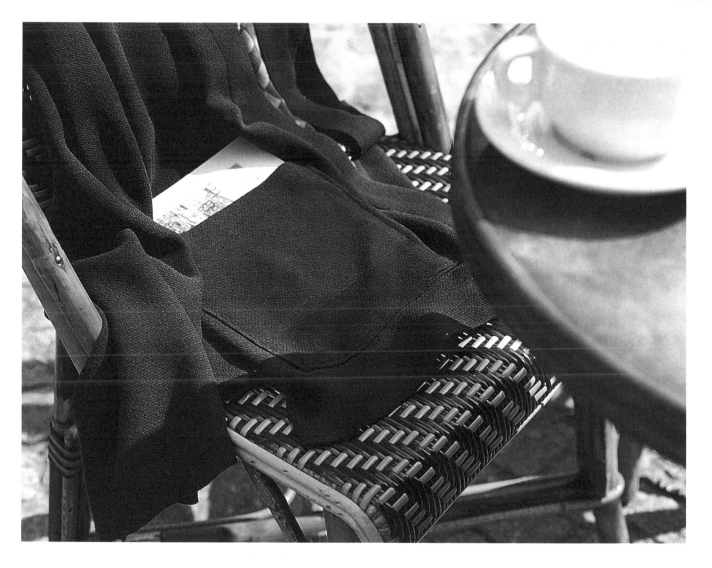

To join on the sleeves

1 With right sides together, pin, baste, and stitch each sleeve to the jacket, matching the center point at the top of the sleeve with the shoulder seam (fig 5, left). Finish the seam by serging or with bias binding.

2 Join each side seam of the jacket and the sleeve seam in one stage, leaving open a 9" (23cm) slit at the bottom edge of the jacket. Press the seam open, and finish the raw edges with serging or

zigzag stitching. Finish the slits at the same time (fig 6).

3 Turn under 5" (12cm) at the bottom edge of each sleeve and machine or slipstitch in place. Fold up into the cuffs.

To finish the jacket

Open out the front band. Trim the hem allowances on the band facings. Turn up a 1" (2.5cm) hem, and slipstitch in place. Slipstitch slit facings. Slipstitch the bottom of the front bands.

pillows

The easiest pillows to make are ones that can be quickly stitched together without the addition of complicated fastenings. To achieve this with style and panache, different fabrics and trimmings can be cut and fitted together with clever seaming or quickly applied with a few sewing machine stitches. Add a selection of unusual and imaginative fastenings and you have the perfect pillow cover.

Triangular pillow

In this unusual pillow, two opposing triangular sections fold over the pillow front and fasten together to hold the pillow form in place. Mix and match plain and striped fabrics for an up-to-the-minute look.

back — 20½" (52cm) · 20½" (52cm) · 12" (30cm)

front — 21" (53.5cm) · 20½" (52cm) · 12⅜" (31.5cm) · **flap**

You will need
¾yd (60cm) plain cotton furnishing fabric, 60" (150cm) wide
22" (55cm) square of striped cotton furnishing fabric
Matching sewing thread
20" (50cm) square pillow form
Button or other decorative fastening
Paper for patterns

To enlarge the pattern
Using the measurements shown left, draw the paper patterns.

To cut out
From plain fabric
1 back
2 flaps
From striped fabric
1 front

To make the pillow
1 Place one flap section to one side of the front piece. Pin and baste together (fig 1). Stitch in from each side for 2" (5cm) only, and press the seam open. Turn under a double ⅝" (1.5cm) hem on the front piece, and stitch in place.
2 With right sides facing, place the remaining flap piece to the opposite side of the front piece and join together. Press the seam open.
3 With right sides togehter, position the back piece over the front piece with with flaps. Pin, baste, and stitch all around the outer edge, taking a ⅝" (1.5cm) seam allowance (fig 2). Trim and and turn the cover right side out. Press.
4 Pin, baste, and topstitch across the cover along the flap edge on the opening side of the front piece and

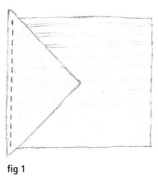

fig 1

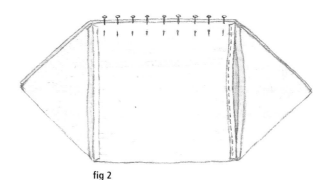

fig 2

along the front piece on the opposite side. Stitch close to the seam lines on both sides.
5 Insert the pillow form into the cover and fasten the two flaps over the front with a button.

Four-cornered pillow

Clever seaming matches the stripes of this pillow together following the shape of the flap so that they meet together at the center when the cover is fastened.

You will need
¾yd (60cm) plain cotton furnishing fabric, 60" (150cm) wide
¾yd (60cm) striped cotton furnishing fabric, 60" (150cm) wide
Matching sewing thread
20" (50cm) square pillow form
Button or other decorative fastening
Paper for patterns

To enlarge the pattern
Using the measurements shown on page 92, draw the paper patterns.

To cut out
From plain fabric
1 front and 4 flaps
1 facing 20½" x 6¼" (52 x 16cm)
From striped fabric
1 back
8 half flap (allow for center joins)

To make the pillow
1 Join the half flap pieces together in pairs, matching the pattern across the central seam line. Press the seams open.
2 With right sides facing, stitch the striped flaps to plain flaps, taking a ⅝" (1.5cm) seam allowance and leaving base edge open. Trim and turn right side out. Press with seams at edges.
3 Stitch a double ¼" (6mm) hem along one long edge of facing. Repeat along one side edge of the front piece.
4 Lay the back right side up. Baste the flaps, striped side down, on each side of the back piece. Place the front piece right side down over the flaps, matching raw edges and the hemmed edge against the seam on one side.
5 Place the facing right side down over the hemmed edge of the front with raw edge matching raw edge of back. Stitch all around. Turn the cover right side out. Tuck the flap inside.
6 Press well. Slide the pillow form inside, fold the flaps to meet in the center and fasten with a button.

Rouleau pillow

Although the front of this pillow looks as though it fastens with tiny buttons, this is just an illusion. There is a back opening similar to the Ribbon-work Pillow on page 96.

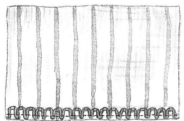

fig 1

fig 2

You will need
¾yd (60cm) of striped cotton furnishing fabric, 60" (150cm) wide
1⅜yd (1.2m) navy tape, ⅜" (1cm) wide
Matching sewing thread
20" (50cm) square pillow form
18 buttons

To cut out
From striped fabric, cut out 2 backs, each 21¼" x 11¼" (53 x 28.5cm), 1 front 21¼" x 14¾" (53 x 36cm), and 1 front 21¼" x 8" (53 x 20cm).

To make the pillow
1 Baste a row of stitches along seam line, ⅝" (1.5cm) from one long edge on the larger front piece. Fold the tape exactly in half lengthwise; pin and stitch the edges together. Form the tape into 18 1¼" (3cm) loops along the long basted edge of the front piece, with the loops facing inward. Check that the loops are evenly spaced and equal in size. Pin and baste in position (fig 1).
2 With right sides together lay the smaller front section over the looped section. Pin, baste, and stitch the fronts together along the looped edge, catching the loops firmly in place. Trim and press the seam open, with the loops facing over the smaller front piece (fig 2).
3 Make the back piece, following steps 5 and 6 for the Ribbon-work Pillow on page 96. Hand sew a button inside each loop on the front to give the impression that it is being fastened by the loop.

95

Ribbon-work pillow   At the back of this pillow, one side folds neatly over an other to form the envelope-type opening, so the pillow form can be quickly and easily slotted inside the cover. The decorative tape is stitching haphazardly around in flower shapes inside a border, creating an unstructured but effective design.

You will need
¾yd (60cm) plain cotton furnishing
   fabric, 60" (150cm) wide
Approximately 11¾yd (10.6m) of plain
   tape, ½" (1.5cm) wide
Matching sewing thread
Tissue paper
20" (50cm) square pillow form
Paper for patterns

To make the pattern
Trace the flower motif on page 97 eight times onto tissue paper.

To cut out
From plain fabric, cut out 2 backs, each 21¼" x 11¼" (53 x 28.5cm) and 1 front 21¼" (53cm) square.

To make the pillow
1 Lightly mark a straight line 2½" (6cm) in from the outer edges all around the front. Beginning at one corner, position the tape centrally over this line, then pin and stitch in place down the center of the tape. At each corner, fold the tape into a loop and stitch down. At the last corner, trim off the tape, tuck under the raw end, and stitch in place.

2 Position the 8 tissue-paper flower motifs inside the outline tape on the front piece, and move them about until they are arranged to your satisfaction. Pin and then baste the motifs in place, basting diagonally across the center of each piece.

3 Cut approximately 1yd (1m) of tape for each flower. Lay the tape over the marked outline, and stitch in place down the center of the tape. Curve the tape carefully around the petal shapes as you stitch, varying their size and shape so that each individual flower will look slightly different.

4 When each flower has been stitched, gently tear away the tissue paper. Cut approximately 6" (15cm) of tape for each center. Stitch in place down the center of the tape, curling the tape around to form a tight circle. Fasten off, tucking under the raw edge.

5 Turn under a double ¼" (6mm) hem on one edge of each back piece, and stitch in place. With right sides up, overlap the hemmed edges of the back pieces for 3¼" (8cm). Pin and baste together.

6 Place the front and back with right sides facing. Pin, baste, and stitch together all around the outer edge, taking a ⅝" (1.5cm) seam allowance. Trim. Undo the basting stitch down the center back, and turn the cover right side out. Press. Insert the pillow form through the back opening.

Pattern diagrams

On the following pages you will find pattern diagrams and cutting layouts for those designs where more than just a simple cutting outline is required. These diagrams complement the instructions given for the wrap-around skirt, drawstring trousers, shirts, and jacket.

Flower motif for ribbon-work pillow

wrap-around skirt

The dimensions on page 46 and the pattern pieces in the pattern diagram (right) are for a size 8. As the skirt wraps over at the front this size will also fit a size 10. To make a larger size add ½" (12mm) to each of the side seams. To make a smaller size reduce each seam by the same amount.

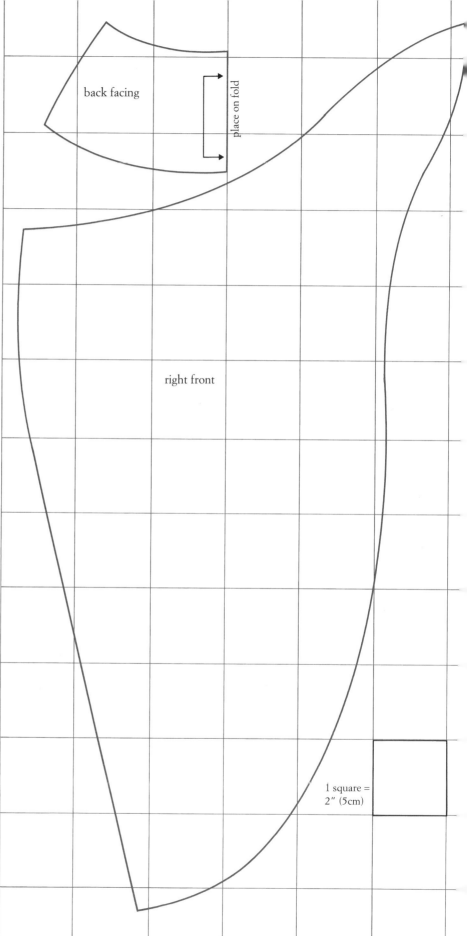

back facing

place on fold

right front

1 square =
2" (5cm)

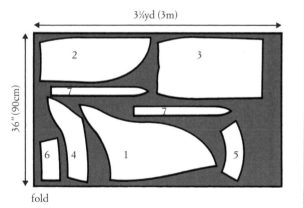

3¼yd (3m)

36" (90cm)

fold

cutting layout

1 right front
2 left front
3 back
4 right front facing
5 left front facing
6 back facing
7 ties

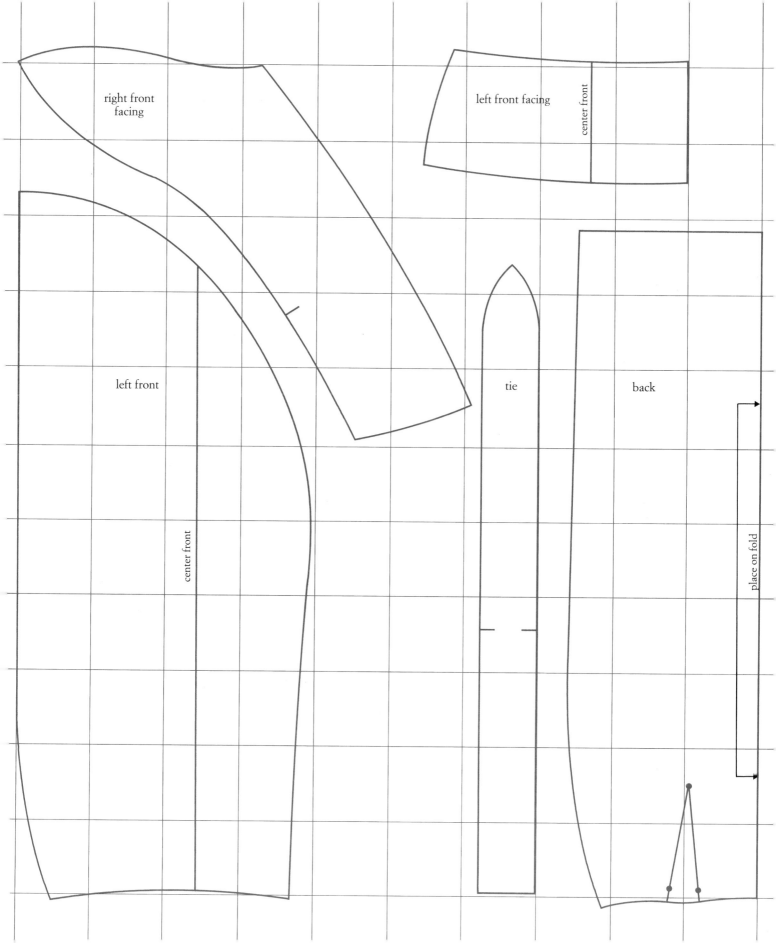

right front
facing

left front facing

center front

left front

tie

back

center front

place on fold

drawstring trousers

The dimensions on page 54 and the pattern pieces on the pattern diagram (right) are for a size 10–12, but because of their loose-fitting shape these trousers should fit most people. Before cutting out the pattern pieces, however, check the leg length as these may need adjusting.

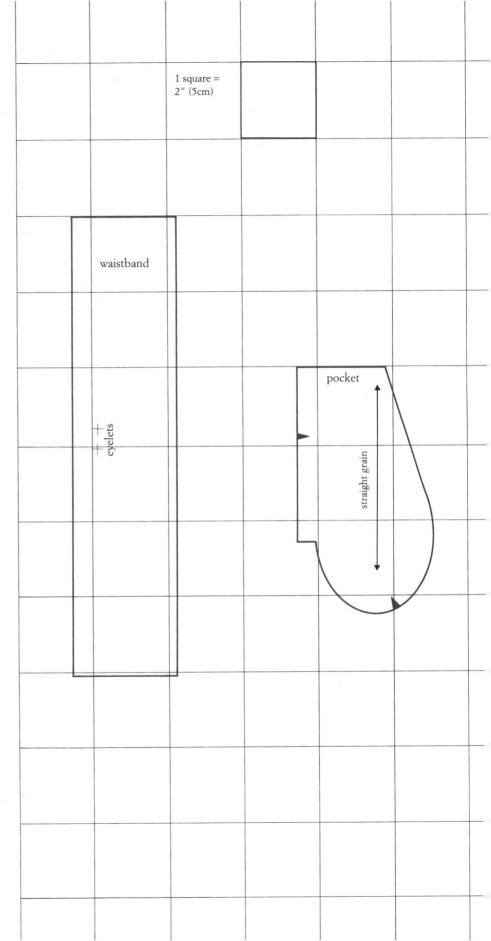

1 square = 2" (5cm)

waistband

eyelets

pocket

straight grain

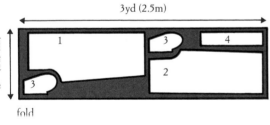

3yd (2.5m)

45" (115cm)

fold

cutting layout

1 front
2 back
3 pocket
100 4 waistband

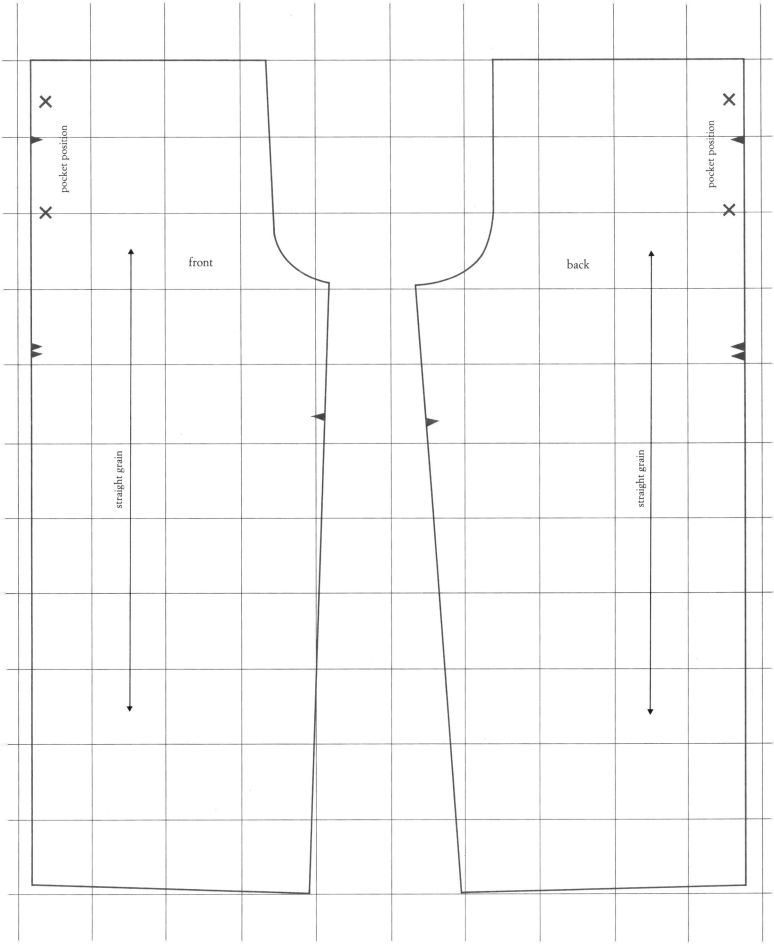

pocket position

front

straight grain

back

straight grain

pocket position

shirts

The dimensions on pages 63 and 65 and the pattern pieces on the pattern diagram (right) are for sizes 10–14. Before cutting out the pattern pieces, check the bust measurement and sleeve length and adjust if necessary. To make a larger size, add ½" (12mm) to each seam or to the overall sleeve length. For a smaller size, reduce by the same amount.

plain shirt   3yd (2.5m)

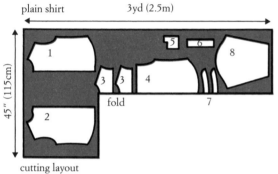

cutting layout

1 left front
2 right front
3 yoke
4 back
5 placket
6 cuff
7 collar
8 sleeve

pintucked shirt   3yd (2.5m)

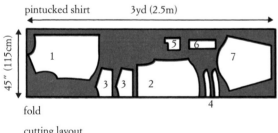

cutting layout

1 front
2 back
3 yoke
4 collar
5 placket
6 cuff
7 sleeve

102

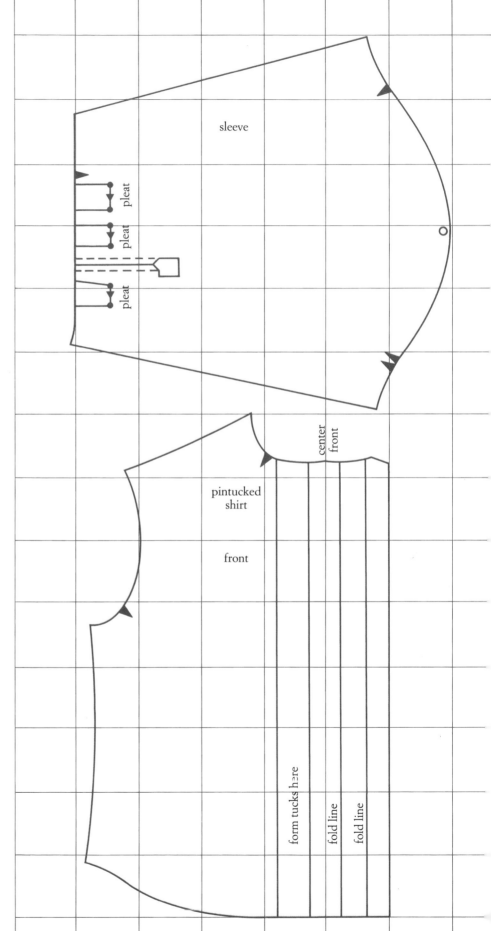

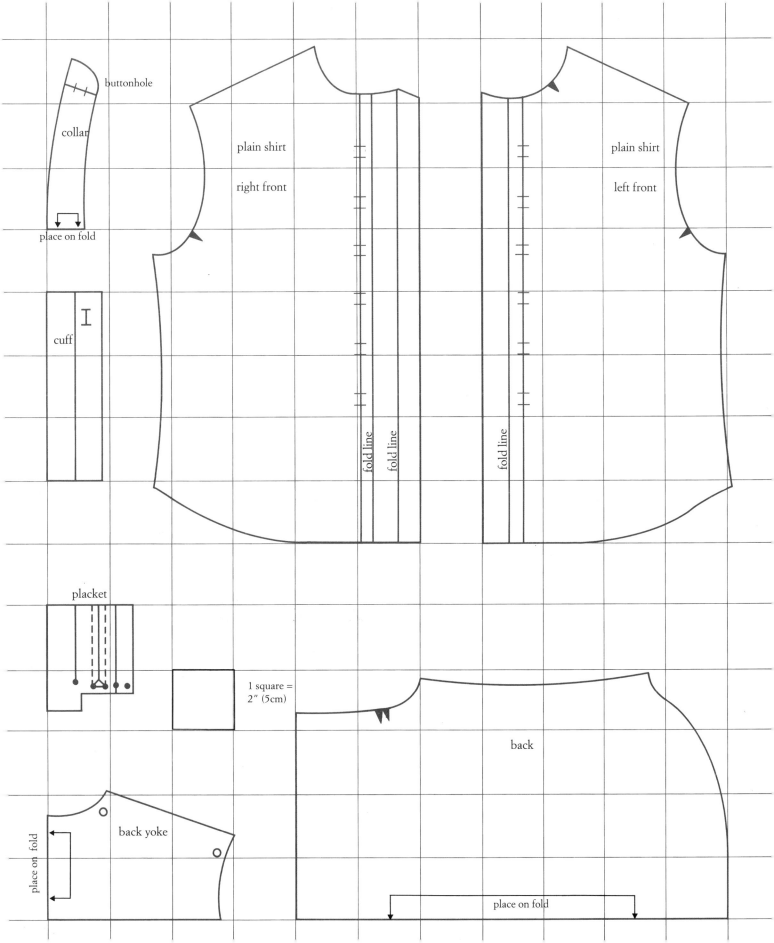

buttonhole

collar

place on fold

cuff

placket

plain shirt

right front

plain shirt

left front

fold line

fold line

fold line

1 square =
2″ (5cm)

back

place on fold

place on fold

back yoke

place on fold

jacket

The dimensions on page 88 and the pattern pieces on the pattern diagram (right) are for size 10–12. To make a larger size add ½" (12mm) to each of the side seams. To make a smaller size reduce each seam by the same amount.

pocket

straight grain

1 square = 2" (5cm)

sleeve

straight grain

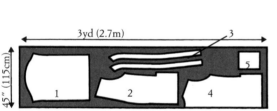

3yd (2.7m)

45" (115cm)

3

5

1

2

4

fold

cutting layout

1 sleeve
2 front
3 front band
4 back
5 pocket

104

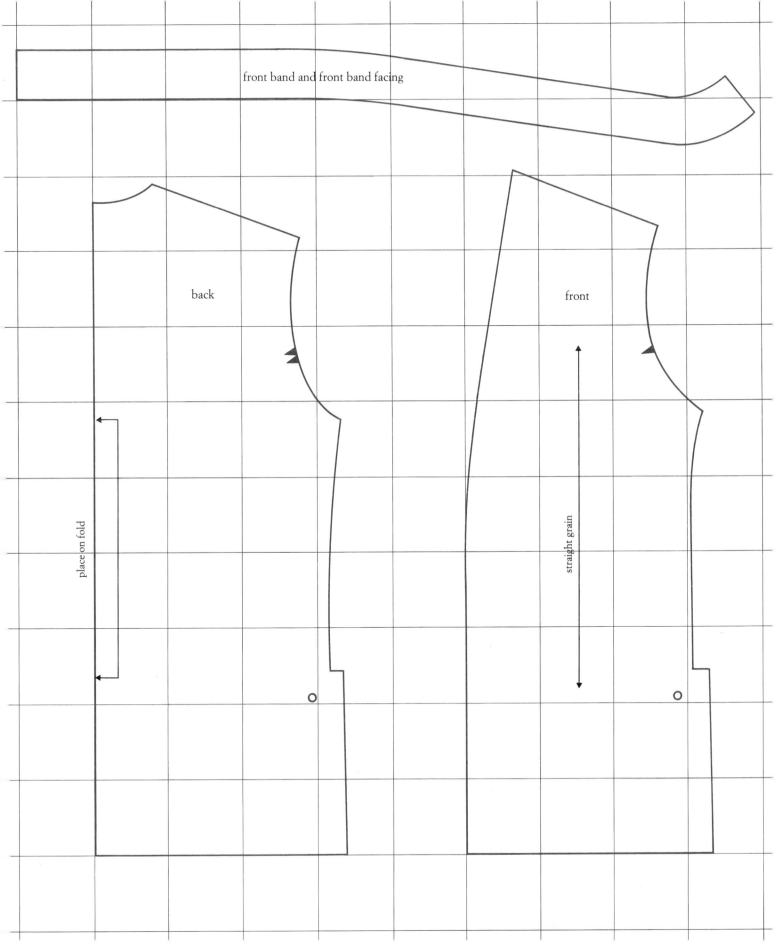

front band and front band facing

back

front

place on fold

straight grain

glossary of fabrics

acetate Made from cellulose. It is often used to make linings.

Acrilan A trade name for an acrylic fabric.

acrylic The generic name for fibers made from the liquid chemical acrylonitrile, which resemble wool and are often used for knitted garments. Acrylic fibers can also be woven.

alpaca The very fine, soft hair of the alpaca – a type of llama – is very expensive and is woven into a luxurious fabric, used for expensive coats and jackets. Because of the high cost, it is usually mixed with sheep's wool for economy.

angora The soft, fluffy hair of the angora rabbit is often used for knitted garments such as pullovers and cardigans.

astrakhan Originally the name applied to the fleece of lambs from Astrakhan, this curly wool is usually black or brown in color and was used to make coats and hats. Nowadays, the term usually denotes a fabric that imitates this fleece and is used to make hats, coats, and collars.

barathea A closely woven, medium-weight fabric made from the finest wool and available in plain colors only. It has a smooth, almost shiny appearance and is used to make suits, skirts, and lightweight coats.

batiste A very fine, sheer fabric made from the finest linen or cotton and used to make handkerchiefs, lingerie, nightwear, blouses, and fine baby clothes.

bouclé A looped yarn which may be woven or knitted into a fabric with a raised, loopy finish that is both attractive and very warm. The yarn can be made from wool or synthetic fibers, or a mixture of the two, and is used to make coats, dresses, and suits.

brocade Originally made from silk, and now from synthetics as well, this fairly stiff fabric is produced on a Jacquard loom. The satin weave appears alternately on the front and back of the fabric to create the design, often depicting flowers or leaves; metallic threads are sometimes woven into the pattern. Brocade is used for evening wear and the heavier types for furnishings.

broderie anglaise Traditionally made in white cotton, with white embroidered eyelets forming the pattern, broderie anglaise can now also be made from synthetic fabrics or mixtures. The white embroidery is sometimes replaced by pastel colors. It is used to make baby clothes, children's dresses, and blouses, and is also available as a trimming in narrow widths for use as an edging or insertion, combined with narrow ribbon.

buckram A stiffened fabric that is used to stiffen belts, hats, and curtain headings. It is available in various weights, the coarsest being made from burlap and the lightest from cotton.

butter muslin A very cheap, loosely woven, fine cotton fabric, originally used for straining milk for butter.

calico A cheap, strong, woven cotton first produced in Calicut, India. It is usually sold unbleached and undyed, when it is easily recognized by its oatmeal-like appearance. Today, dyed versions are also available. Calico is often used in home furnishings or to make dressmaking toiles.

cambric A fine, closely woven fabric made from linen or, more usually, cotton. It has a slightly glazed surface on one side and is usually available in plain colors. It is used to make baby clothes, night wear, and blouses.

camel's hair Originally the name for a very expensive and luxurious fabric made from camel hair, and often mixed with wool for economy. It is very soft but also very light and warm, and is used mainly to make coats. The term is now also applied to thick, camel-colored woolen fabrics.

candlewick A shaggy, loose-piled fabric produced by pulling tufts through a loosely woven base fabric. Generally made from cotton, candlewick may now also be synthetic, and is used to make bedspreads and bathrobes.

Cashmere The hair of the Cashmere goat is woven into this most beautiful soft, fine fabric, recognized by its smooth, silky finish. As a yarn, it is knitted into luxurious pullovers and cardigans. The fabric is very light yet also very warm, and is used mainly to make men's and ladies' suits and coats. Extremely expensive, it is often mixed with sheep's wool to reduce the cost.

cavalry twill A very strong woolen fabric with a twill weave, now sometimes made from acrylics. It was originally used to make riding breeches and is still in demand for hardwearing trousers.

challis Made from fine wool, this lovely fabric is light in weight and suitable for making dresses and shawls. It is available in plain colors or printed.

chambray A soft cotton fabric with a colored warp thread and white weft. It is similar to denim, but much lighter in weight and not as strong, and is very often pale blue in color. Chambray is used to make shirts, dresses, and children's clothes.

chamois A very soft leather cloth, usually tan in color, made from the skin of a small mountain goat. Fabric is sometimes woven to imitate it and is given the same name.

cheesecloth A loosely woven, rather rough cotton cloth which was originally used to wrap cheeses. As a fashion fabric, it is more closely woven and can be dyed. It is used to make flimsy trousers and dresses and is very inexpensive.

chenille With a hairy pile all around, this yarn derives its name from the French word for "caterpillar." It can be made from a variety of fibers including silk, cotton, wool, viscose, and various mixtures. The yarn is often used for knitting; when woven, it has a thick, velvety pile and is usually used for soft furnishings, but also occasionally as a fashion fabric.

chiffon A very soft, very fine fabric originally made from silk but now also from synthetic fibers. It is available in a wide range of usually plain colors, sometimes with graduated shading known as "ombre." Chiffon drapes beautifully and is used for making scarves and soft, floaty garments.

chino A firm, closely woven cotton fabric with a twill weave, originally used for summer uniforms for the armed forces. Often still available in army khaki and beige, it is very durable and is used for making trousers and casual wear.

chintz Traditionally a cotton fabric printed with a large design of flowers or birds and sometimes glazed with a special finish, chintz is used to make curtains and slip covers. Nowadays the term is also applied to glazed cotton fabrics in plain colors, and these too are used mainly for soft furnishings, especially scatter pillow covers.

ciré The name derives from the French word for "waxed," and the original fabric was indeed waxed to give it a shiny finish. Now the term is used for fabric that has been treated to provide a shiny finish. These fabrics are often water-repellant and have a smooth, slippery feel.

cloqué Cloqué is the French word for "blistered," which exactly describes the appearance of this fabric. Originally made from silk, it is now also produced from synthetics. Cloqué is used to make dresses.

corduroy A cotton fabric recognized by the velvet ribs running along its length. These vary in thickness, with the widest ribs being known as "jumbo cord" and the finest "baby cord"; "needlecord" is slightly heavier than baby cord. These are strong, hardwearing fabrics and are useful for making children's clothes, as well as skirts and trousers for adults. Although corduroys are most often produced in plain colors, needlecord is sometimes printed with attractive designs.

cotton Produced from the seed pod of the cotton plant, cotton is processed into many different fabrics which vary greatly in quality and cost.

cotton jersey A knitted cotton fabric, originally used mainly to make T-shirts and underwear, but now also used for skirts and dresses. Thicker types are used to make sportswear.

crêpe de Chine A luxurious fabric, originally made from silk but now also from synthetics. It is woven using a twisted yarn, which produces the characteristic crinkled surface. Available in plain colors or in beautiful prints, it can be used to make blouses, dresses, and beautiful lingerie.

cupro The name is short for cuprammonium rayon, a soft, silky fabric which is very good for lining. It is sometimes sold as Bemberg silk or Bremsilk.

denim Taking its name from Nîmes in France, where it was first made, this very strong fabric has become universally popular for jeans, jackets, and shirts. Traditionally made with a colored – usually blue – warp thread and a white weft, it is often dyed, disguising this effect.

devoré velvet This fabric has been chemically treated to remove, or "devour," some of the surface of the velvet, leaving a pattern in the remaining pile. As some of the velvet has been removed, the resulting fabric is light and drapes beautifully. It is used for scarves and evening wear.

Donegal tweed Originally made in County Donegal, Ireland. Made from wool, it has a speckled effect, the specks being surprisingly bright in color; used for suits and jackets.

douppioni A silk fabric with a slubbed effect in its surface. Often wrongly referred to

107

as "wild" or "raw" silk, it is very popular for making wedding dresses, bridesmaid's outfits, and ballgowns. It is surprisingly inexpensive and is available in a huge range of colors.

drill A very strong twill-weave fabric, originally made from cotton but now often with synthetics added. It is usually made into overalls and other working garments.

Egyptian cotton A very fine-quality cotton which is exceptionally smooth to the touch. It is used to make good-quality bed linen, nightwear, and baby clothes.

flannelette This is a cotton fabric with a nap produced by brushing the fibers to produce a warm, soft fabric that is used to make nightwear and blouses.

foullard A soft, printed twill-weave fabric, originally made from silk but now also from synthetics.

gaberdine A very closely woven, strong and slightly stiff twill-weave fabric that can be made from wool, cotton, or synthetics.

georgette A very fine, filmy fabric, similar to chiffon but woven with a twisted yarn to give it a slightly crinkled surface. It is usually made from silk and is used for garments and scarves.

gingham A checked fabric, in which the checks have been formed by the weave. It is usually made in white with one other color, resulting in checks in three tones. Strong and durable, gingham is usually made from cotton but sometimes from synthetics. It is relatively inexpensive and has an attractive fresh appearance, giving it many uses, but it moves in and out of fashion.

habutai A fine, soft, relatively inexpensive silk used for lining, and also for making shirts

Harris tweed A rather rough tweed woven by hand in the outer Hebrides, a group of islands off the coast of Scotland, of which the Isle of Harris is one. As it is made on hand

looms, the fabric is only 27" (69cm) wide. It is very durable, lasting for many years, and is used for making coats and sports jackets with a country look.

lambswool A very soft, fine wool taken from lambs before they are seven months old. Lambswool is often used in high-quality knitwear.

lamé A fabric woven from metallic threads, usually with another fiber which might be silk or synthetic. It is used for evening wear.

lawn A very fine fabric, usually made from cotton but also from linen. It is slightly crisper in feel than batiste, and is used to make blouses, shirts, and dresses, as well as children's clothes.

Liberty prints Beautiful, exclusive designs printed on cotton, silk, and wool by Liberty of London.

linen Produced from the stem of the flax plant, this fabric is used for table and bed linen and fashionable garments.

Lurex The trade name for a metallic thread which can be woven into fabric or knitted, or used as a sewing or embroidery thread.

Lycra The trade name for an elastic fiber. These fibers are used where stretch is needed in swimwear, tights, and figure-hugging fashion garments.

madras A cheap cotton from Madras, India, which is hand woven into brightly colored checks. The colors are obtained from vegetable dyes and tend to bleed and fade when washed.

melton A very firm, closely woven wool fabric with a short nap. It is used for making coats and suits.

merino Some of the best-quality wool is obtained from the Merino sheep. The name is now sometimes applied to a good-quality woolen fabric.

mohair Produced from the long hair of the Angora goat, mohair fabric tends to be hairy, but is very warm. It is often mixed with wool to make cloth suitable for suits.

moiré A finish given to silk and acetate fabrics to produce a watermark pattern.

net An open-mesh fabric where the yarns are knotted rather than woven or knitted. It can be made from silk, cotton, or synthetics, and various densities and degrees of softness are available.

nun's veiling Originally used for religious purposes, this has now become a fashion fabric. It is made from fine wool with an even weave, to create a delicate fabric which can be used to make dresses and blouses.

nylon A synthetic fiber produced from mineral sources, it is extremely hardwearing and very strong.

organdy A very fine cotton fabric with a crisp finish, often confused with organza which is the silk equivalent. It is used for interfacing and for party dresses and hats.

organza Very often confused with its cotton version, organdy, this is a very fine but stiff, crisp fabric with a lot of body. Originally it was made from silk, but synthetic versions are now available. It is used as an interlining and interfacing, as well as for making ballgowns.

Orlon A trade name for an acrylic fabric.

ottoman A distinctive fabric with wide ridges running across its width, making it quite stiff. Originally made from silk, it is now more likely to be synthetic and is used to make evening wear.

panné velvet A velvet fabric in which the pile has been pressed flat in one direction, giving it a very shiny, slippery appearance and feel. It is usually synthetic and is used to make evening wear.

percale A fine, closely woven cotton fabric which has been given a smooth finish. It is widely used to make bed linen and shirts.

Pima cotton A very fine, good-quality cotton fabric used mainly for making shirts.

polyester A popular synthetic fiber, it is versatile and can be used in many different ways. It is often mixed with other fibers such as wool and cotton.

poplin A much-used fabric made from mercerized cotton yarn. It has a slight sheen. It is heavier than lawn and durable; polyester is sometimes added to make it more crease resistant. Poplin is available in plain and printed versions and is used to make dresses, blouses, children's clothes, and much more.

ramie A strong, durable fabric made from a vegetable fiber extracted from ramie grass, which grows in Asia. Ramie is sometimes used to make hats and in dress fabrics when mixed with other fibers. Also called China grass.

satin The name of a weave which gives a smooth, shiny effect on one side of the fabric. It can be made from almost any fiber. Satin has many uses depending on the basic fiber.

seersucker A fabric with alternate bubbly and tight stripes, which are formed when the fabric is woven and will not iron out. It can be made from cotton or nylon and is used for dresses and children's clothes, and moves in and out of fashion.

serge A durable, medium-weight twill-weave fabric available in plain colors only. Used for suits and trousers.

shantung A medium-weight silk fabric with a slubby texture that is popular with the fashion conscious for dresses and suits.

silk Produced by the silk worm, this beautiful fabric comes in a great variety of forms. Used for curtains and soft furnishings, wedding dresses, ballgowns, and day wear.

spandex A polyurethane fabric with a lot of stretch, and therefore used extensively for making swimwear and underwear – in fact, for any garment that requires stretch.

taffeta Originally made from silk, and now often from synthetics, this is a crisp fabric with a characteristic rustle. Usually produced in brilliant plain colors, taffeta is used to make evening wear and wedding dresses.

Terylene A trade name for polyester.

tulle A very fine net with tiny holes, which is used mainly for making wedding veils.

velour A closely woven, heavyweight woolen fabric with a smooth finish, which is used for making coats. The name is now often used for velour jerseys, which are stretchy knitted fabrics with a velvety pile, often made from synthetics and used for casual clothes.

velvet A fabric with a cut pile which can be made from cotton, synthetics, or silk, each having its own characteristics. It is used to make garments for special occasions.

vicuna Produced from the vicuna llama of South America, it is an expensive and luxurious fabric.

viscose A type of rayon made from cellulose, the quality of viscose has improved over the years. Can be used on its own to make skirts and dresses or mixed with other fibers for greater versatility.

voile A fine, lightweight fabric, now made mainly from cotton or synthetics. It is used to produce lightweight, floaty clothing.

Wool Produced from the fleece of the sheep, wool is a very warm and practical fabric used for winter garments.

109

index

acknowledgments

The author would like to thank Hilary More for her hard work and patience and for writing the instructions for the curtain, pillows, gussets and pillowcases and for organising their making up; the team at Quadrille; Liberty of London for their generosity in supplying so many of the fabrics; Mary Telford for making many of the projects; Alice Butcher and Lyn Holt at Liberty for their support; Diana Vernon for her encouragement; and my long-suffering family for their understanding.

The publisher would also like to thank Liberty plc and the other companies listed below for their generous help in supplying fabrics:
Liberty plc (pages 29,31,47,53,62,64,89); Bennison (page 42); Calver & Wilson (page 83); Nina Campbell (page 11); Designers Guild (pages 45,57); Malabar (page 69); Ian Mankin (pages 13,73,93, 96); Mulberry Home (page39); Osborne & Little (pages 11, 86); also Beryl Miller for making additional projects and Sally Harding for her invaluable editorial assistance.

The publisher and photographer also thank Richard Lowther and Lynne Robinson, Lucinda Ganderton and Emma Williams, Amanda Hawkins Knitwear Design, Damask, Diana Digby Ratafiat Hats, Gainsborough Silk Weaving Co. Ltd, Hobbs, Millside Forge, Nina Spooner.